D0869177

Rocky Road
to
RECOVERY

Breaking the Generational Curses of
Family Dysfunction and Self-Destructive
Behaviors through Faith and Action

Trust God, but Do Your Part...

A MEMOIR

KSENIA K.

First Printing 2021
ISBN 978-1-7367330-0-4

I would like to dedicate this book to my mom, my husband Chris, and my son Noah. Our families have been stricken with patterns of self-destructive behaviors, and I am hoping to break that cycle, with God's help, so that I do not pass it on to future generations.

This book is a tribute to God for opening up my eyes at the right time and guiding me towards achieving sobriety of mind, body, and spirit. It is an ongoing process, but I firmly believe that with God, all things are truly possible.

This book is for everyone who is afflicted by self-destructive behaviors; all those who were raised and had been affected by people in their families suffering from affliction; mothers and fathers crying for their children; children crying for their parents; wives and husbands crying for each other–anyone grieving for their loved ones.

CONTENTS

ACKNOWLEDGEMENTS

I WOULD LIKE TO thank Angela McClain, my editor, who reached out to me after two years of silence after the original idea for this book was born, and reminded that God was waiting for me to write my testimony.

Special thanks to my friends who took the time to read my manuscript and gave honest and helpful feedback, and their continuous support.

I'm grateful for Father Gabriel who always believed in me, helped me make the first steps towards life recovery and still provides spiritual support when I need it.

My husband, Chris, is always there for me, and I'm so incredibly thankful for his love and patience when I act a little out of it (or a lot!). You are a blessing. I love you!

Noah, my two-year-old, brought a whole new meaning to my life and shows me what kind of relationship parents and children should really have. Noah gave me an ultimate reason to break the vicious cycle of dysfunction for good. Because of him, my heart is full of love, and my soul is full of hope.

I'm thankful to God for not letting me perish. Not only He raised me up from the "dead" and redeemed my life, but He also gave me a new life of purpose.

I'm thankful in advance for all the people who will support me after the book is published. I expect there will be some who will turn their backs on me after learning about my past, but as someone once said, "There are people who will lift you up, and there are those who will try to bring you down, because that's just what they do! You can't win them all." To those who end up rejecting me, that's ok, but please use my story to come out of your own denial, find your own dysfunction and work on putting a stop to it. You'll be surprised how much we might actually have in common.

God bless!

INTRODUCTION

*R*OCKY ROAD TO RECOVERY is my personal story, followed by lessons learned and action steps towards recovery from self-destructive behavior patterns. I do not mean it to be professional advice, but that which got revealed to me during the process. The idea behind the book is that we need to meet God halfway and "work out our salvation" together. God is merciful, but we have to ask for His help first, listen to His voice, and take action based on His guidance.

I divided this book into two sections. Section One has two parts: my life before finding God and after. Section Two is the steps I took and lessons I learned during the process of life recovery. If my personal story is of no interest to you, you can jump right into Section Two. If you are only interested in my story, then read Section One only. For a complete picture, it is best to read the entire book, from beginning to end.

I hope that you, the reader, whether you are afflicted yourself, or are related to someone who is afflicted, realize that there is hope, even if it doesn't seem that way at the moment. God is powerful to create change in anyone's life. We can start with prayer and believe that change will happen; then we keep praying and wait for God's answer and take action. If you are someone who lost all hope—this book is for you. If you are someone who is already going through the process of life purification and transformation, this book will serve as encouragement to keep going.

I asked my parents and got permission to share some gruesome details about our family's past. This was the hardest thing for me to do. I got really depressed after bringing those memories back and almost gave up on finishing the book, because it was so incredibly painful. I thought I got over everything long time ago. In reality, all the trauma was buried deep inside my soul, heart, and body. Writing it all out brought every memory back with unexpected intensity, but I know that it will serve to bring true healing. I felt like I was a teenager again and experienced all the described events all over again. My mom and I still have a lot to figure out; I am going through the process of learning true forgiveness towards my parents. I did not put all those details out in the open in order to condemn my parents, but to show how generational dysfunction and alcoholism played out in all of our lives, and how it can easily be passed on to next generations.

Please be mindful that this is my very first book, inspired by God, and I speak from my heart. If you see any mistakes, or if my views differ from yours, kindly forgive me. This has been quite a journey!

God bless!

Ksenia K.

FOREWORD

There is a curious episode in the Gospel of Mark. A group of people brings a blind man to Jesus and asks Him to heal the man. Jesus then takes the man outside the village and anoints his eyes with spittle and asks him, "Do you see anything?" The man responds, "I see men; but they look like trees, walking." Jesus then lays his hands on the man's eyes again and the scripture says, "He looked intently and was restored, and saw everything clearly." (Revised Standard Version, Mark 8:23-25). This account in Mark is remarkable among the Lord's miracles because it shows there is a process to healing. The blind man goes from complete blindness to having distorted vision to ultimately seeing everything clearly. This pericope

tells the same story, albeit in a more compressed fashion, that Ksenia K. tells in her remarkable narrative Rocky Road to Recovery. In Rocky Road to Recovery, we see Ksenia K.'s transformation as she goes from spiritual blindness to an ongoing and expanding sense of the Lord's presence in her life, which is true sight.

Among the many remarkable aspects of this story, there are two points that are the most important. First—Christ's love for Ksenia. We read and weep about Ksenia's traumatic childhood and her descent into chaos, but always in the background of her suffering— there is Christ. His loving presence is revealed in various ways: through an old prayer book, a television program, or finding an Orthodox Church in the ghetto—all strange and unexpected occurrences that point to the providential care of our Lord for Ksenia. Secondly, Ksenia K. is defined by her courage. Almost at every phase in her life, Ksenia demonstrates the fortitude to change her situation. She has the bravery to leave her native country to come to America. Once in America and faced with the false promise of making money, she has the daring to keep going until she can earn enough money to make her mother's dream of owning an apartment come true. Finally, Ksenia's most courageous act is to respond to Christ's call to change. Like the blind man from the Gospel of Mark, Ksenia's transformation has been a process. Although getting sidetracked at times, Ksenia has kept going in her commitment to the Lord. The Lord continues His steady presence in her life as He gives her greater and greater clarity about her purpose in life. The Lord has bestowed on Ksenia the blessings that come from a faithful life. She now has a family and a career. She is a faithful member of her church leading a life of integrity.

Whether or not you are struggling with addiction, Ksenia's story is worth your time. Her story teaches us that the Lord is always present in our life. Like Ksenia, our job is to respond to His call with courage and to stay faithful to Him through all the ups and downs of life. We know that true sight comes only through having Jesus Christ at the center of our life.

Father Gabriel,
an Orthodox priest.

PROLOGUE

How in the world did I get here?

*After everything that happened… how am
I still alive and well, living a normal life?
How did I get out of that mess?*

This must be a dream...

Wait, no… This is reality!

*I am a 36-year-old woman from Russia,
living on the beautiful coast of South
Carolina in the United States of America, in
a nice, big house, married to the love of my
life, raising the most amazing toddler. I hold
a Bachelor's degree and have a stable job.
My faith is stronger than ever. Life is good. I
have many dreams, and I set goals to make
them reality.*

It wasn't always like this...

Here's my story.

SECTION ONE

I

CHAPTER ONE

Mom

I BECAME EXTREMELY ANGRY. I did not have control over my emotional state. My miserable situation at home did...

Wait, let me rewind.

I was born in the city of Kazan in 1984, still Soviet Russia back then. Even though Kazan was always one of the biggest and most populated cities in Russia, and most people lived in government supplied housing, my living situation differed from the rest of the folk. The government was supposed to provide mom with a normal apartment, like it did for everyone else, but that never happened, and we ended up living in a tiny studio apartment that used to be a storage unit to keep strollers of the tenants that occupied our apartment building.

My first childhood memory of my father is when he was standing in the hallway of our studio apartment. Mom was holding me in her lap. It didn't seem like they had much to say to each other. TV was glaring in the background. My mom was trying to put me to sleep because it was late. Dad cheated on her with one of her best friends.

Mom never really slagged him, but I know he liked to drink and was quite a loser. He never paid child support. Mom became a single parent just a year after I was born. I recollect seeing him only one more time in person. He also called me on my sixteenth birthday and wanted to meet, but I refused because he was just a stranger to me, and I didn't have any desire to deal with another alcoholic in my life. Now, as an adult, I wish I could see him and let him know I'm not mad at him, but mom said he might be already dead. If he is, it makes me sad. Who knows how he felt all these years. What if he was lonely, and no one loved him? Perhaps I will never find out.

Mom was a beautiful, talented, smart, and artistic woman. She was a professional ballet dancer and could have had a distinguished career. She got an offer to be in the main role in "The Nutcracker" and move to Czech Republic to pursue her career, but she decided to stay home, got married and had me. Mom loved my dad, but he betrayed her. I guess that was the first stage in her downfall. Later on, mom became a dance instructor. She taught ballet and all types of dance to children and adults, including teaching dance in my school. I was in her class and always felt special and happy to be my mom's daughter. She had her own dance team. They traveled around the city and performed in front of enormous crowds. She was a local star. They featured her in the newspaper. I remember how proud I was of her. She was happy with her life and career. She felt like she was fulfilling her potential.

As a child, I traveled with her and took part in all kinds of performances, whether it was dancing, singing, or acting. I started acting when I was very little. Every year we performed at a traditional New Year's event for kids. Every year it was the same fairy tale, and I progressed from being a snowflake to being Father Frost's (Russian Santa Claus) granddaughter, which was a big deal for a kid. That said, my childhood was really magical. Not having a dad did not seem to hurt me at all. I never felt that anything in my life was missing. I loved my mom. I adored her. I was super proud of her. I wanted to marry her. I didn't need anyone else besides her, and I know she loved me too–I always felt it. We were always together. I never thought all that could change drastically.

It all started when my mom got laid off from her job. Her dance team fell apart. She did not travel around the city and perform any longer. She had to find another job and forget about her true calling. I believe that's when her soul started to die, little by little. Only when we lose something, we realize how much we need it in our lives.

Eventually, mom got a new office job and made new friends. Those friends loved to get together and drink after work. Even though I have seen my mom drink with her dance friends before, I witnessed nothing negative that happened, or maybe I was just too young to understand, except that one time when I found out all the adults, including Santa and my mom, were drinking before New Year's performances for kids. There is even a joke in Russia that Santa is not a Santa if he is not drunk.

As I got older, I started noticing that she came home a lot later at times, and the way she behaved was different. I could tell there was something going on. I guess mom became lonely. She started dating and brought men home periodically. I witnessed a few relationships that she got into. A couple of those guys that she brought home ended up staying, and they stayed for a while, and I had to share space with them. One guy was twelve years younger than her, liked to drink and was abusive. Another guy was even worse, besides being super ugly. They drank together all the time, and I just followed them around (because mom brought me everywhere with her since I was still young) and observed all the atrocious behavior. I was always disgusted and ashamed by them. I thought, *why in the world my beautiful, talented, amazing mom would be with these nasty, disrespectful, abusive men…* I didn't understand it at all.

Now, let me tell you about the place where I grew up. It was a very tiny studio apartment that was not suitable for a child and two adults to live together. There was no shower. We had a tiny black-and-white TV, foldout couch (with storage underneath where I kept all my books–my "treasures"), fridge, old desk for kitchen table, sink, two-burner electric stove, and a handmade wooden twin bed for me. We didn't have a dining room table, so when it was time to eat, we would put a stool in the center of the room and a piece of plywood on top to serve as dinner table. Since we lived on the first floor, we had to put a metal cage on our window so that no one could break in from outside. Older kids often threw stones and dirt at our window. We were that "abnormal" family that everyone hated and made fun of.

My bed was located right next to the foldout couch where my mom slept, so when she brought someone home, I slept pretty much next to them. And I was a girl who was growing up to be a young woman. Even though I never felt like any of those men were looking at me weirdly, I can't tell for sure. Sometimes I heard my mother having sex with the man she was with; when she thought I was asleep. I always hated it. My mom never talked to me about sex. She never mentioned or apologized about having sex with her partner in front of me. I always pretended that I was sleeping, but I really wasn't.

My heart was pumping, and I could not wait for it to stop.

I did not have any personal space. I did not have my own desk, a corner to hide, or another room to run to. Gosh, I didn't even have a real bathroom! Privacy was nowhere to be found. So most of the time, I had no choice but to sit on my bed, listen and watch, no matter what was happening in front of me. Not to mention, I also witnessed drunken debauchery, cussing, fighting, and verbal and physical abuse regularly. Often, my mother and her partner would binge drink for two weeks at a time, if not longer. In those times, I would come home after school, clean up after them (sometimes puke), open the window so that the smell of alcohol and cigarettes would go away, and hope that I wouldn't have to do it again the next day. If I came home and they were not there, I would try to do my homework as quickly as possible, and sit there, terrified, waiting for them to come home.

I was a good kid–polite, nice, helpful, and caring. Mom raised me right and certainly instilled some wonderful qualities in me I am still grateful for. I was an excellent student, and I tried to do well in school, even amid all this chaos and nervous breakdowns.

Eventually, that nice kid became a very, very angry one. I lost all respect for my mother, and I hated our studio, and I was so embarrassed, so embarrassed, that I always kept my eyes down when I was coming out of the building. I did not want anyone to look at me, even though I knew that every neighbor boy was staring at me (local boys liked getting together in front of our door!). This is how I became insecure, and this is how I lost my self-worth. Those tender years, when my mother should have been the most nurturing, became the most destructive to my future. It created a lot of problems for me as a young adult. It made me lose love for my mom. It made me lose myself. It made me lose trust. It made me lose love for myself.

But see, I can't blame mom for everything. She didn't have it easy either. She grew up with a father who was a full-on alcoholic, and two brothers who also were alcoholics. Only her mom–my grandmother–was sober and responsible. Mom went through a divorce, raised me all on her own in a tiny studio without a shower (try to take care of a baby with just a small sink, no dishwasher, washing machine, and cloth diapers these days!) She had a difficult relationship with one of her brothers. I remember it vividly when he beat her up unmercifully. I don't know what happened between them before that, but I recollect standing outside of the bathroom (at his house), where he locked her up and beat her. I was crying and begging to let her go for what seemed to be forever. I was still very young and felt so powerless to protect my mom. She could barely walk afterwards and had a severe concussion and a black eye. I could not believe that my favorite uncle, who I absolutely adored, was capable of such violence.

Mom didn't have any positive male influence in her life. That's possibly why she ended up in dysfunctional relationships and thought that was all she deserved. Losing her dream job was also a big hit. Being stuck living in the studio for over twenty years didn't help either. I heard her say way too many times how much happier she would be if we lived in a normal apartment. I saw her cry many times when she was tipsy. I hated seeing her cry, but I could tell she was really depressed. Years were passing by and nothing was changing for the better.

CHAPTER TWO

Grandparents

M Y GRANDPARENTS HAD four children, one of which passed away, born premature. They were married for over fifty years, but I never saw them hugging or kissing, or saying *I love you*. Grandma wanted to divorce grandpa, but uncle Slava stopped her. Grandma was always unhappy and said hateful words about grandpa, wishing for him to die. I loved my grandpa dearly. He took me for nature walks and tobogganing in winter, played board games with me. We went to the marketplace together, and he always bought me ice cream.

That's when he was sober.

As I was growing up, more and more often, grandpa came home wasted, and he either verbally fought with my grandma, or went to bed. He slept in a separate room that smelled like booze and urine. I had to cover my nose when walking in if I needed to grab something from there. Grandpa spent a lot of time in his shed. He was an alcoholic, and his shed was his hiding place. Sometimes he stayed there for a few days at a time. Grandma would send me there to check on him and tell him to come home. I would find him sitting there, wasted, with a bottle of vodka, or sleeping, and sometimes his pants were wet from peeing himself. As a teenager, I yelled at him and shamed him for doing this to my grandma. In reality, it made me sad he chose to drink instead of spending time with me like he used to. Grandpa passed away first, when I was already living in the United States. I was heartbroken. It was the first death in our family. I was miles away and couldn't be there for his funeral. I still loved him and did not feel any hatred or resentment—just deep sorrow. Something died in me when he died. I cried a lot. I wish I could say goodbye. Even though my grandma wished him death, she told me she missed him after he was gone. She felt very lonely. She died from lung cancer not too long after grandpa's death. I couldn't be there for her funeral either.

Grandma was the strongest woman I have ever met, but kind and sensitive at the same time– big heart. She suffered a lot from her husband's behavior and all three of her children. All of them drank. Grandma always took care of me, and I took care of her. When I stayed with her, she washed my clothes, cooked delicious food, made my bed, and helped with money. I did grocery shopping for her, gave her bath, mopped floors, dusted, and washed the windows. We loved each other dearly. She was my only stable rock in life, and the only sober person in my life. The thing is, my grandma was paralyzed in one leg. She stayed inside for many years without stepping outside at all. She lived on the fifth floor of an apartment building that had no elevator and wasn't able to use the stairs. She was literally stuck in her apartment. The only way for her to have fresh air was to go out to the balcony and watch what was happening on the street, five stories below. That's exactly why I had to take responsibility and run errands for her, even when I wasn't staying there. Taking care of her taught me how to take care of myself. I didn't have a normal life of a teenager, but I sure learned how to be an adult at a young age.

Grandma loved me very much, but she did not want me to be on a dance team that I joined as a hobby. Dancing, acting, and singing always made me the happiest. I took that after my mom. Grandma didn't support mom's profession of a ballet dancer in the past, because she thought it was useless. Remember, grandma grew up during war times, when bread winning was the only concern. She would say to me, "You will end up like your mom!" Mom, on the other hand, was happy that I was following her footsteps and was developing my artistic talents. My mom and my grandma had a difficult relationship. They were very different. I stayed with my grandma a lot because of drinking parties at my house. Only after grandma passed away, my mom started feeling sorry about drinking and not taking care of her own mother. I guess we all have our own hurts.

Uncle Slava died on the street as an unknown person. He was a real piece of work. He stayed at grandma's once in a while, for days or weeks at a time. If he didn't drink, he would sit in his armchair and read all day. On the days he drank, he would come home yelling and cussing at grandma, calling me a rat when I tried to defend her, and threatening to throw me over the balcony. He was tall and strong, so I naturally was pretty scared of him. Quite often he would roam the streets, looking for his alcoholic friends and disappear for a while, not contacting my grandmother. She would always feel worried and wait for him to call or come back home. Uncle Slava gave me my first cigarette. One day, he tried to touch me "down there." I only realized what he tried to do a lot later when I remembered that day. That memory is sickening. When I went to his grave years later, I wanted to spit on it, and I felt he deserved to die on the street as an unknown person because of who he was. My mom told me I should not keep any resentment towards him, but I never told her what he tried to do to me.

Between my house and my grandma's, I felt stuck, and I didn't even fathom of getting away from my alcoholic family. Ever...

But one day, I did.

I ran.

I ran away. And I swore I would NEVER be like my mom!

Technically, I flew. I flew to America—the country of opportunities. The place where all your dreams come true!

CHAPTER THREE

Stepdad

I FIRST MET MY stepdad when I was around twelve years old. One day I came home and found a guy hanging out with my mom. *Just another dude,* I thought. Then he was there the next day, and the next day. Then suddenly he was there every day. I met his mother and his son, who was the same age as me. At first, everything seemed great. We would go to his mother's house and have dinner. I made friends with his son (who is also an alcoholic now). I saw that my mom seemed happy, and little by little, he became a part of our family. Finally, we had some stability.

However, it didn't last long.

Eventually, he started coming home drunk on a regular basis. My mom and him worked together and finished work at the same time, but often he would come home a lot later. If he were drunk, he always started arguments. Not one time we had a peaceful evening. He was a completely different person when drunk. Sober, he would sit at home and watch TV and barely say one word to me. Drunk, he was like a devil coming out of darkness. As time went by, drunken arguments often turned into physical fights. I started getting worried for my mom. Periodically, she would have a black eye and missed work, and I was the one who was sent out to talk to her boss and make up an excuse why she couldn't be at work.

I was always on mom's defense. In the beginning, stepdad did not touch me at all. A lot of times, he would physically abuse my mom, but wouldn't touch me even if I tried to jump in. A fight started happening often. I would sit in our studio apartment, scared, listening to footsteps. I just wanted to be invisible. If I realized that he was approaching the door, I would sit on my bed in a fetal position, barely breathing and trying not to start a conversation with him, even though it never really worked because he always found a reason to start a conversation with me. If he were sober, it was okay, and I felt relieved, but that changed from day to day, and I was in a permanent state of anticipation of chaos.

As if that wasn't enough… my mom started drinking too. They would go on binge drinking periods, have constant fights and cuss, drink and smoke in the studio. There was only one tiny window to let fresh air in, no air conditioner, or fan, or anything like that. I had to breathe cigarette air constantly. No wonder I was sick often. From time to time, they would invite friends over to share a bottle of vodka with them. Sometimes those friends would even stay over when there was already no room in our studio apartment. I even witnessed some friends having sexual intercourse right in the middle of the room on our floor. At some point, mom started being nasty to me, acting like I was in their way, calling me names and acting like she didn't care whether I was there. I was not her little girl anymore. When she was hungover, she would send me to the store to get beer, or if there was no money, she would send me to the pharmacy to get medicine for her that contained enough alcohol for her to feel better. It was so humiliating. Oh yeah, and I also had to clean up puke from when she passed out drunk on my bed. That's when I first started feeling hurt deep inside. I already worried for her being hurt by her boyfriend, but now I was also afraid to lose my mom.

Many times I would try to run to the police station, but had to turn around, being scared that my stepdad, still only mom's boyfriend at that time, would physically harm her or me for telling on him. Domestic violence was seemingly okay in Russia. It happened all the time. We lived on the first floor right in front of the elevator (originally, that tiny studio was used to keep the tenants' strollers in, and that's why there was no shower!) Local boys would often spit on our door and stick matches in the lock so that we wouldn't be able to unlock the door. It wasn't rare that I was locked out of the studio. We didn't have phones back then, so I had to wait outside, hoping my parents would come home soon. Everyone who came into the building heard everything that was going on inside our studio. Our neighbors would always listen to us fighting and did nothing. Often, I would run to my friend's house, scared, bawling my eyes out. I was always afraid to come home and find my mom hurt, or worse—dead.

When I got a little older, I stopped being so afraid. I was just super angry. I experienced my first genuine hatred towards someone. I hated my stepdad so much that I wasn't even afraid to hurt him physically. One time when he kicked my mother in the stomach (and it was something I have never seen before), I grabbed a bottle of vodka and smashed it on his head. He lost consciousness. Mom started screaming and crying. He was bleeding out of his head. I felt like it was revenge. I was not afraid. I was enraged.

One other time, he pulled out a can of paint and poured it all over the floor. Then he took all of our clothes (the only clothes that we had because we were poor) and dumped and smeared paint all over it. So we had no clothes to wear. Then he grabbed both of us by the hair and pushed us on top of the paint, dragging us all over the floor. Somehow I got out and managed to grab him by his neck. My adrenaline was rushing so hard that I squeezed my hands around his neck very, very hard, ready to strangle him. He started choking, so I knew it was working because he stopped his grip on my body. My mom started screaming, "Stop! You will kill him!" And I screamed back, "I want to kill him. I hate him!" After he came to his senses, and after I let go of my grip because I didn't want to spend my life in jail, I knew he would do nothing else that night, so I got dressed and got ready to go to my friend's house. He was sitting on the floor, smiling, with his middle finger up, as if letting me know that there would be payback.

Another memorable moment was when it was a New Year's evening, and my mom and I made some traditional holiday salads and beautifully decorated our studio. We were waiting for him to come home, hoping that the night would be magical. As soon as he got home, we realized that the night would not be magical, but a night of terror. He was wasted and started an argument right away. He was getting nastier and nastier, and I knew that there would be a fight again. He said he wanted to have sex with mom when he gets home, but I was always in their way, and I was the reason they fought so much. He also told me I should serve him hand and foot when he is home, and that he is in charge of the house. I got my diary out and started writing all of my feelings of hatred towards him because I needed an outlet somewhere. He saw me writing something, and a few days later, he found my diary and read everything I wrote about him, where I called him names and said how much I really hated him. I was stripped of the last piece of privacy I thought I had. Two days later, he came home when my mom wasn't there. I was sitting on my bed, ready to go to my friend's house. Next thing you know, he grabbed a cutting board and slammed it on my head, breaking it in half, saying, "This is for what you wrote about me, bitch!" Thank God, I was wearing a hat, and it didn't hurt that much. I felt so humiliated and deeply hurt. I started crying and asked how he could treat a teenager like that, especially a girl. I was miserable. I ran to my friend's house and cried all night. I did not know what to do, where to go, and how to get out of that life.

I was so embarrassed by my family and the poverty I lived in, so unhappy and broken, and felt so ashamed, that I didn't even try to date anyone, thinking no one would ever want me.

I can say though that I did have some great friends. My best friend never turned her back on me and let me stay at her house all the time, even though her own dad was drinking. At least we had each other and used to hide in her room if her dad came home drunk. These kinds of friends are hard to find these days. My dance team friends were truly awesome. They accepted me the way I was and made me feel comfortable. They didn't care what I wore and where I lived. I'm thankful that I had some healthy relationships in my life.

There were periods of sobriety. Those were peaceful moments for me. I was not particularly happy, but I was at least okay that our house was quiet. I prayed a lot. I prayed on the corner of my bed, especially during fights. I would keep repeating the same prayer over and over again—the only prayer that I knew. My heart throbbed with pain.

I think one of the major things that made me lose all respect for my mother was when I found her and her boyfriend passed out drunk, naked on my bed on New Year's Day! New Year is the biggest holiday in Russia. That's when Santa Claus comes and leaves presents under the tree after midnight. And that was my present??? That handmade bed was literally the only thing that was specifically made for me. I had nothing else of my own. I felt so dirty, so disgusted, so hurt by the fact that they didn't even think that it was inappropriate and really didn't care about how I might feel about it, that I just turned around and left. But before I left, I wrote them a letter, expressing how nasty they were and how dirty, low, and embarrassed they made me feel. I had every intention to never go back home. How? I didn't figure that one out yet. A few days later, they came knocking on my friend's door, asking me to come home. They were sober. Even though they asked me to return, they didn't seem to regret what they did. They said it wasn't such a big of a deal, and that I should get over it. My feelings didn't matter. I ended up coming home, but there was no way back mentally and emotionally.

Soon after that, I asked my mom if she wanted to choose him or me. I wrote her another letter. She told me that she had to stay with him because she didn't want to be alone, and that I would understand only when I grew up. This was a big **** I still don't understand, years later. I felt like my mom betrayed every part of me. She broke my heart. I didn't have a dad. I only had my mom, but then I lost her too. Even though I still deeply cared about mom, I lost all respect and affection for her. I thought she would end up dying on the street, and I would be parentless completely. The only feelings that I had left in me were bitterness, deep sadness, anger, and resentment. I was numb to everything else. I hated my stepdad for ruining her life and mine. No matter what he did to her, she would always take him back. I meant nothing...

At some point, I finally got involved in a "relationship". I was 16, and my boyfriend was 31. And guess what? He loved to drink! He would be super sweet to me, if sober, and I mistakenly felt like I was in love with him. I felt protected because he was older and had a job. Then he started letting me try alcohol, and we ended up drinking together. I felt like I was living a glorious life. I had my first sexual experience with him that did not include actual sex. I felt all grown up. I felt like I had some security and pain relief, which, of course, was false.

After a couple of drunken fights, I realized I did not want to get into the same lifestyle as my mom and my stepdad. I broke up with my boyfriend. He tried to get back with me, but I was very firm and said no. I was glad I did. I started thinking about ways to get out of the house I was living in.

I can't say that I never thought of running away or jumping off the bridge.

I think it's important to note that my stepdad also came from a dysfunctional family. His parents were also divorced. He got married and had his son, but his wife left him and the baby, and he ended up being a single dad. He didn't handle it very well. My guess is that when he was drunk and abusive, he took it out on mom because he was mad at his ex-wife for leaving him high and dry, but I can't tell for sure.

What a vicious cycle of dysfunction and brokenness…

God heard me finally! I overheard my friends talking about an opportunity to go to America for the summer and earn some money. My mom's biggest dream was to have an actual apartment. I thought maybe I could help her by going to America, making money, and purchasing an apartment. Maybe everything would change.

Maybe they would stop drinking, and she would finally be happy. Maybe she would love me again. See, my friends didn't think I would go through this program because I was poor, and they knew what was going on in my life at home. They didn't even suggest for me to go to the meeting where they would talk about this program. My feelings were a bit hurt, but I said that I was going to listen to what this program entailed anyway, and then I would decide if I could go through with it or not.

The program sounded very expensive. I definitely didn't have that kind of money. I didn't even know if I could ask my parents for money because there was no stability with them. I figured it would take me almost a year to make enough money to pay for the program. And that it did. I begged my parents to help me. I promised to buy them an apartment. I got two jobs while I was studying at the university. I was working a night shift in a jazz bar as a waitress, and then went straight to school and often fell asleep at my desk, and on my days off, I would work as a ticket collector on a bus. I was able to save some money, plus my uncle gave me some, plus, with a lot of arguments and fights and almost losing hope that I could ever go to America, mom and her boyfriend actually came up with the rest. With God's help, I collected enough money to apply for the program. There it was. My ticket out. More on that later.

CHAPTER FOUR

Big Plans, Not Real Opportunity

M Y PRIMARY GOAL for going to America was to buy an apartment for mom. I worked very hard to get a visa. Until the very last moment, I thought I would not get approved. I got a phone call on the very last day they were giving out visas, with the confirmation that I was going. I felt like a winner!

When I finally came to America in 2003, it was the middle of July. I was supposed to go back home on the first of October. That meant that I only had two-and-a-half months to make enough money to buy an apartment. That was unrealistic. I got a job at Morey's Pierce in Wildwood, New Jersey, as a ride operator of Kiddie Swings. Wildwood seemed like paradise to me, comparing to where I came from. I loved the ocean, and I loved Morey's Pierce Amusement Park. It just seemed so unreal. I felt very lucky to be working there, because in the past I only saw these kinds of parks on TV. My hourly wage was $5.65 an hour. I lived in a motel room with five other students. We shared beds together. I ate Ramen noodles and hot dogs almost every day. But even after trying to save every penny, I only had seven hundred dollars to take back to Russia with me. My trip to America cost me twenty-five hundred, so that seven hundred was not even enough to cover that, and forget about buying an apartment, or anything.

In Wildwood, I met another J-1 student. We decided to get married and apply for political asylum. Dima didn't have big plans like I did. He wasn't serious about life. We filed our application, but he was too busy binge drinking and partying, and he never showed up for court, which automatically disqualified him from being eligible for asylum. All that took about three years. I ended up filing for divorce and was placed in deportation proceedings. I felt like a total failure, but didn't have any other choice but to accept the fact that I would have to go home with nothing. I would have to go back to my broken home where I had no future. The judge gave me four months to leave the country. I felt defeated. As the day of my departure was approaching, I met Steve (not the real name) at the bar where I worked. He sat quietly at the bar and seemed bored. I came up to cheer him up and inquire what he was up to. He told me he was in the Air Force, stationed in Hawaii. He came down to visit his parents and got bored sitting at their house. He seemed really nice and very calm. I was single at the time. I was invited to go to New York for my friend's birthday party next day, so I invited Steve to go with me. He gladly agreed, and we drove to New York and had a blast. I think he liked the spontaneous, wild side of me. He was quite the opposite. I was 22, and he was 29. One of my biggest dreams was to visit Hawaii. Steve invited me to come visit, and I didn't think twice. *Might as well*, I thought. *I will be going back home very soon and will never be able to see Hawaii or the US in the future.* I barely knew him, but I found a ticket and put it on my only credit card. About a week later, I was there! I must say, my decision-making skills were not the best. I wasn't afraid of anything at all.

Steve was nice and treated me very well. We had a great time, and he suggested we date for real. I had to tell him I was going to leave the United States in just a few weeks and never come back. He convinced me to stay in the US, and we got married on a Hawaiian beach later that summer when I came back to Hawaii. Sounds like a fairy tale! You would say, *what else would you need*, right? I had a nice husband who loved me, offered stability and took good care of me. What was missing? Well, at first, things were okay, and we seemed to be happy, but after we moved to Charleston, SC, he got deployed the first time, and then when he came back, he got deployed the second time, and then he got deployed the third time. We never really spent any time together to really get to know each other. After a couple of years of this, I wasn't sure he was the right guy for me. It just didn't seem we had much in common. We stayed married for seven years. My timeline might be a little off because it seems so long ago, so please forgive me if something is not completely clear.

While my husband was deployed, I felt bored and lonely. I started going out with everyone from work. As soon as my night shift was over, we all would party somewhere. There was no shortage of people who would provide a party. Little by little, it became a habit, habit without which I could not live. Sitting at home and watching TV was super boring for me. I wanted to be out and about. I wanted to be seen. I wanted to feel accepted. When my husband was home, we were fighting because I went out all the time. Sometimes he would go out with me, but he would sit at the bar and sip on a beer without talking to anyone. I thought he was extremely boring. He embarrassed me. I started resenting him for not being as "fun" as I was. If he tried to say something to me about my excessive partying, I would just get mad. At some point down the road, he told me I needed to seek help and that the military could provide some counseling for me. I got angry when he said that. I was in denial. I thought I was living my life to the fullest and there was NOTHING wrong with me. I was so blind. Notice how I was recreating chaos that I was used to growing up. Normal life just didn't seem that exciting. Yes, I physically left my home in Russia, but mentally I was still in the same exact place. I brought my family's dysfunction with me.

It took me a few years, but I saved enough money working at nightclubs to put down for a mortgage deposit. I called my mom and asked her to find a place that she wanted to buy. She found a two-bedroom apartment, and I sent her money for the deposit, which was fifteen thousand dollars! That kind of money was unheard of back home. That's how my journey down really started. Yes, she bought the place, but I had to send her a thousand dollars every single month for the next fifteen years, besides trying to provide for myself. The pressure of working nights was huge (no, I wasn't a prostitute!). I thought that was the only way for me to make enough money. I wanted to reach my goal. If I missed the payment, mom would lose the apartment. I wasn't giving up on my plan. I was really determined and chose to ruin my soul (*not that anyone cared anyways*, I thought), but I had to make sure that mom was taken care of. Not sure if I did it because I loved my mom so much, or I was extremely co-dependent and thought that the apartment would buy me her love back… I really think it was both.

CHAPTER FIVE

Coming Out of Denial

I WAS IN DENIAL that I had a problem for a few years.

Between my failed marriages, I dated DJs and bartenders. They provided music and booze. I always felt like I was the life of the party when I had enough alcohol in my system. I felt like this other person, who had been hiding deep inside, was coming out at night. I was a serious introvert when sober. When drunk, I was confident, fun, fearless, loud, and entertaining. That "liquid courage" definitely worked, and I liked feeling different from the way I felt without it. I had to have at least three drinks to get myself out of my shell, but once the right amount of alcohol kicked in, it was on. I was careless and absolutely nothing bothered me. Alcohol made me worry free, so to speak. I could finally relax and not be consumed by painful thoughts and memories.

Eventually, recreational drugs came about. I never wanted to try them and usually would say no, but my best friend convinced me to try just one time, promising it would be so much more fun. That night I think I tried everything they had at the party. My fake eyelashes were falling off my eyes, and I could barely talk. I stayed up all the next afternoon. Thanks, friend!

You know now, when I think back to my early twenties, I almost feel like it wasn't me who did all these things, but someone else. It's crazy how one person can change so much.

Little by little, party life became the way of life—the only way I knew how to live. I had no major responsibilities, except my mortgage payment every month, no parents, no kids. There was no one to guide, control, or stop me. My parents had no idea what I was doing, and I was very comfortable with that. They were miles away and probably could not care less if I told them—they were drowning in their own dysfunction.

Going back to my marriage times. My husband and I moved to Charleston, South Carolina. Parties continued. New people, new parties. I was never alone. I always had a partner in crime with me. People who didn't drink seemed super boring to me. I thought they were missing out on real fun. I spent most of my money on food and alcohol. I didn't even care about clothes or jewelry, like any other normal girl would. As long as I paid my bills and had a place to stay, I was ok.

Even though I was baptized as a child and used to believe in God, party life eventually sucked anything that had to do with faith out of me. I mocked God by saying things like, "I don't believe there is an old man in the sky who is in charge of my life and everything else." Clearly, the devil was doing his work.

In reality, I just wanted to fit in and be accepted by everyone. A few years passed by and alcohol started getting me in more trouble rather than providing fun. I got kicked out of a couple of bars for being annoying. I fell asleep behind the wheel—once, while driving on a bridge, another time—driving home, with a police car behind me. Somehow I didn't get killed or pulled over. I truly believe my guardian Angel was there for me this whole time!

I thought I hit my rock bottom when I got a DUI. I spent almost three days in a filthy jail—cold, hungover, exhausted, starving, smelling like crap. Nonetheless, after my husband finally bailed me out, I took a shower, napped, and headed straight back to a local bar. I could not stop talking about how crazy and "funny" people in jail were. Seriously? I mean… they kind of were, though.

My husband begged me to get help, but I was still in total denial. Even though deep inside I was ashamed of getting a DUI, I still didn't think I had a serious problem. The idea of quitting fun and living a boring life was not attractive to me. I realize now that alcohol was my God—it gave me wings, so to speak. Without it, I didn't feel like a person worthy of any attention and love. The real, sober me wasn't good enough. I didn't think about my future. In fact, I would say, "I was born to party. I'm so good at it. I will not have a career until I'm at least 40!" Kids were not even discussed.

DUI wasn't my lowest point. It was John who I met when I visited Myrtle beach, SC, after I finally separated from my husband. I didn't know he was on probation from drug charges. We drank together, but nothing else. One evening, a year after we met, I noticed he wasn't acting like himself. I found out his probation ended, and he immediately got coke. I hated that new person. He wasn't himself. He scared me. We got into a huge fight. I yelled at him for putting himself at risk of getting in trouble again, but he didn't listen to me. I actually ended up moving to Vegas in hopes of starting a new life, but only stayed for a month and a half. Vegas was definitely not a place to start over! What was I even thinking? My purse with my money, green card, credit cards, and social security card in it got stolen, so I literally had to jump in the car and drive for three days back to Myrtle Beach with nothing! I had only a few pennies left in my pocket. I was back with my boyfriend and had nowhere else to go and no money. Then my car broke down, but I had no money to fix it. I was stuck!

My boyfriend and I would have heated arguments often. One night he hit me. I called the cops. He went to jail. I had a black eye for the first time in my life. Now I was in the same position my mom was years ago. I recreated my family's dysfunction to a T! I got stuck living with an abusive boyfriend who was also an addict, and I thought that was my fate.

Slowly, but steadily, I was getting sick of the misery that was my life. I was like a lost ship in the sea—no direction or hope. Something had to change. I didn't know how or where to start, but the thought was there. One day I managed to get to a local church. All I knew was that I needed God back in my life, and that I had nothing to offer, except my broken soul. I cried throughout the whole service. I couldn't even tell why. And I was hungover.

SECTION ONE

II

"Things do not change; we change."

—HENRY DAVID THOREAU

Psalm of Repentance

Have mercy on me, O God,
according to Your great mercy;
According to the abundance of Your compassion,
blot out my transgression.
Wash me thoroughly from my iniquity
And cleanse me from my sin.
For I acknowledge my iniquity,
And my sin is always before me.
Against You only have I sinned
And done evil in Your sight;
That You may be justified in Your words,
And prevail when You are judged.
For behold, I was shapen in iniquity,
And in sins did my mother conceive me.
For behold, You love truth;
The unclear and hidden things of Your wisdom
You have made clear to me.
You shall sprinkle me with hyssop,
And I will be cleansed;
You shall wash me and I will be
made whiter than snow.

You shall make me hear joy and gladness;
My bones that were broken shall greatly rejoice.
Turn Your face away from my sins.
And blot out all my transgressions.
Create in me a clean heart, O God,
And renew the right spirit within me.
Do not cast me away from Your presence,
And do not take Your Holy Spirit from me.
Restore to me the joy of Your salvation,
And uphold me with Your guiding Spirit.
I will teach transgressors Your ways,
And the ungodly shall turn back to You.
Deliver me from bloodguiltiness,
O God, the God of my salvation,
And my tongue shall greatly rejoice
in Your righteousness.
O Lord, open my lips,
And my mouth shall declare Your praise.

CHAPTER SIX

Finding God

I WAS BAPTIZED AS a child in an Orthodox Christian Church in Kazakhstan. I visited churches here and there, but it was never a big part of my life. My grandmother told me she prayed for everyone before bed, but no one even taught me the Lord's Prayer, or much else about my faith. I saw pictures of Jesus in the children's Bible, but it was just another book of stories to me. I enjoyed visiting churches, but never stayed for the service.

I was first introduced to Jesus when I was about 8 years old by my mom's friend, who was a Baptist. She gave me a few booklets to read and a mini prayer book. She was so kind and spoke about Jesus in such a warm way that I naturally got very interested in Christian faith and immediately started using my prayer book. I memorized the main prayer and used it every day and every time I was having a hard time. My little heart was open to God.

One day my wallet where I kept my mini prayer book got stolen on a bus. I was so heartbroken. The good thing was that I knew the prayer by heart and could continue praying as usual. The prayer came in handy when mom and stepdad were fighting. I prayed that drinking and fighting would stop. The only way for me to survive those terrifying nights was to repeat my prayer over and over again, until I fell asleep, if at all possible.

As my life in America was becoming more and more fun, God was on my mind less and less often. A good friend noticed my spiritual need and took me to an Orthodox Church in Philadelphia. The rules didn't impress me. I was told I could not ask for a prayer for anyone who was not Orthodox. I thought it wasn't right. I left the church that day and decided that religion was not for me because it had too many rules, and I was not planning on coming back. And that's where the evil one took a hold of me... I only understood that years later.

Nightlife became my God. I felt like I was on top of the world. Life was full of fun—I had many friends, no responsibilities, and no one to answer to. I was FREE! Or so I thought. In reality, this was the beginning of my descent into doom. My soul was in the devil's hands.

And there I was, standing at Saint John's Greek Orthodox Church in Myrtle beach, SC, years later, hungover, tears streaming down my cheeks. I did not understand what was being said and sung. Half of the service was in Greek, but I didn't even understand any of it in English. I never stood through the whole service before in my life. I probably reeked of booze, but no one seemed to pay attention. When it was time to take Communion, I walked up sheepishly, embarrassed, not really knowing what I was supposed to do. Later on, I came in to get some holy water and ended up talking to the pastor. He was very inviting and told me I could come back anytime.

I didn't go back to church after that. God allowed me to hit my lowest point first. I had to move out of the place where I lived at the time before I could get in more trouble. Thankfully, I had a friend who still accepted me for who I was and lent me a helping hand. I moved in with her. Soon God gave me the first sign...

CHAPTER SEVEN

God's call

O NE DAY I was cleaning and listening to The 700 Club program on TBN Christian network. I wanted to learn more about God, but wasn't sure where to start. I didn't have a Bible or any Christian friends. Suddenly, the story on TV caught my attention. I stopped what I was doing and sat down in front of the screen. It was a true story about a prostitute who got kidnapped and locked up in a basement. She was scared and desperate, so she cried out to God, "Please Get Me Out of here! If you set me free, I promise to never go back to my profession, and I will be your witness to the rest of the world!" God heard her. Someone was passing by and heard her scream through a tiny basement window. Help was immediately called, and she was set free. She never went back to being a prostitute, but started helping other women in that field understand that they needed God, and they, too, could become free. It became her life mission. She succeeded and helped many lost women come out of darkness and see the Light.

The story resonated with me so much, for some reason, and my heart was beating so fast that I had to chug a glass of water. I took this as a sign! At the end of the program, the anchor provided a phone number and invited people who were watching to call and accept Jesus into their lives. I never really believed in that and felt kind of weird, but something told me to make a leap of faith, pick up that phone and call.

The first question they asked me was what my relationship with Jesus Christ was at the moment. I said there was none. The lady with a very soft and caring voice read a prayer with me and asked me if I wanted to accept Jesus back into my life. It was too late to back off, so I reluctantly said yes, without truly believing. Even though I didn't fully believe in what I had done, the evil one weakened his grip on me the moment I said yes, and that's how I got a new start in life.

CHAPTER EIGHT

First Miracles

ONE OF MY roommates happened to be studying at a Bible school at the time. I asked her if she had an extra Bible. She had plenty and gladly handed one to me. I started reading. It was definitely not an easy read. I read a few verses at a time.

Soon John and I moved to a small apartment in the middle of the ghetto. Life wasn't pretty there, and I fell back into old habits. That was the only way I knew I could cope with the misery. John and I fought a lot. He wanted to smoke weed and barely worked. He never had any money, and I practically paid for food, rent, and utilities (in addition to my monthly mortgage payments). I was always broke, and I hated it. I resented John for not being a man enough to find a stable job and help me with bills. He was a good guy at heart, but a complete loser in life, and I was right there with him. I knew that wasn't going anywhere good. I didn't really have a choice though (or so I thought), so I stayed and continued building resentment towards him, our way of life, and myself. We were totally co-dependent! I had a total victim mentality and thought that he was the only reason we were not doing well, but I wasn't really looking for solution either. I knew something had to change; I just didn't know where to start and how to get through the day without feeling miserable and hopeless.

Then the biggest miracle happened! Just a few blocks away from where we stayed, I noticed a small church. To my biggest surprise, it was Saint Nicholas Orthodox Church! *What? There is an Orthodox Church in the middle of the ghetto where I live?! How is that even possible?* First of all, Orthodox churches are rare in America. Second, that wasn't a suitable area for it. Third, it was Saint Nicholas Orthodox Church. My grandmother gave me a beautiful charm with Saint Nicholas on it when I was little, and I loved it dearly, until it disappeared one day, which made me very sad. I immediately knew that God heard my prayers and was inviting me in. I also knew in my heart that Saint Nicholas himself was protecting me this whole time! Considering I did not have a car, it was quite miraculous that the church was a walking distance, and there was no excuse not to go visit. So I did.

I gathered enough courage one day and went in. The church was tiny and cozy. Everyone was very kind and welcoming. I stayed through the whole service, but this time I didn't cry, and I wasn't hung over. I paid attention and listened carefully to every word. I loved being there. It was so peaceful and calming—not anything like all the nightclubs and bars that I was used to. At the end of the service, the pastor came up to me and asked me some questions about where I was from and what brought me there. Next thing you know, right when I was about to leave, he got a beautiful study Bible from the For Sale shelf ($40 price tag!) and just handed it to me, saying, "I feel like you need this!" I didn't know what to say and left in awe, promising to come back. God came through again. I knew it in my heart.

The study Bible was exactly what I needed. It explained what different passages meant. I read it carefully, trying to understand every word. The more I read, the more it was speaking to me on a deeper level. I came back to Saint Nicholas and tried to follow the service book, reading into every word. I loved it. I felt like there was hope for me, finally. Only one thing was missing. I still had a hard time believing in Jesus. I believed in God the Father, but Jesus—I was still not sure about. I wanted to believe in him so badly, because I wanted to experience faith in all its fullness, that I remembered my childhood prayer from my mini prayer book and started praying fervently. I was asking God to help me believe in His Son again, just like back in the day when I was still a child.

I went to church every Sunday and every day during the week that I was able to attend. I felt like something was pulling me back there, and I started wanting to fill my days with church, Bible reading, and prayer. God was doing His wonderful work in me. I still cared about John and wanted him to change his ways too. I brought him and his eight-year-old daughter to church once or twice maybe, but he wanted to sleep in on Sundays, and when I gave him the Bible, he read one page and literally fell asleep. The evil one wasn't having it with him. He never let him go. I kept going back to church by myself, Sunday in, Sunday out. My mind and my soul slowly started changing. I quit drinking all hard liquor, smoking cigarettes and stopped going out. I stopped hanging out with certain people and tried to spend more time at home reading the Bible instead. Even though I didn't stop drinking completely, I started seeing the difference in how my mind worked. I was thinking more clearly and finally had the motivation to get up in the morning.

One day, someone suggested I try singing in a choir. I thought it was ridiculous because I wasn't much of a singer, but gave it a chance, anyway. There are no musical instruments in Orthodox churches. Everything is chanted or sung a cappella. To my surprise and everyone's, I did really well in the choir, so I got invited to sing regularly. Little by little, I fell in love with the church music and chanting. The main chanter recognized my talent and took me under her wing. I became her protégé, so to speak. She was in her sixties; two of us together made a beautiful duet. We sang and chanted at every service, at baptism and funeral. I finally felt truly needed and fulfilled. I miss those days. My mentor moved away. Gradually, I was falling in love with the Orthodox faith and its traditions and holidays, its singing and chanting, its beauty and depth. The more I learned, the deeper my desire to learn more grew.

I started believing in Jesus...

Time came for the house blessing, when the pastor comes to his parishioner's house, reads prayers, walks around the house and blesses it with holy water. By that time, I started wearing the cross that my grandmother gave me years ago and was already washing my face with holy water I brought home from church; we truly believe in the healing powers of holy water in the Orthodox Church. Even though I was embarrassed by the apartment where my boyfriend and I lived, I still wanted to have it blessed, hoping it might help us somehow, so I invited the pastor to come over. My boyfriend wasn't home when he came. Immediately after blessing the house, Father Gabriel turned to me and said, "Get out before it's too late! This is not the way to live.

You are made for so much more!" When I heard that, I felt like he only confirmed what I already knew, because deep inside I believed it. I wanted to leave, but didn't know how or where to go...

God showed up again.

Two days after Father Gabriel's visit, I got a random phone call from a friend of mine who asked me if I wanted to rent a room from her. I knew it was my call to action. I immediately agreed, packed my stuff, and left John two days later. I tried to help him, but he kept going down instead of up. I had to make a choice and help myself first.

Three years later, I got a phone call.

A mutual friend informed me he passed away because of a drug problem.

I could easily end up there too.

I'm forever grateful to God for sending me Father Gabriel. And I'm grateful to myself for listening and taking action.

I moved to my friend's place and finally had a nice, clean space of my own. I started praying every morning, afternoon, and evening. I read books about the lives of Saints, (yes, I'm a believer!), and I wanted to be more and more like them. I made my first attempt (and there were several) to quit drinking and could finally start saving some money. Since I didn't have a working car, I asked people from church for rides to make it to service every Sunday. I went to alcohol classes so I could get my driver's license back. I began learning about the effects of alcohol to my body and mind. My thoughts and behavior were changing. I was waking up from the dark mind fog slowly, but steadily. Things were looking up. After the longest time, I felt hopeful again.

I started getting more familiar with the services and prayers of the church. My desire to learn more and dive deeper into faith led me to the next step that made all the difference. I met a young woman at the church. She was about my age, and we quickly became friends. She told me more about Orthodoxy and introduced me to the sacrament of Holy Confession. Confession seemed super scary. Just thinking about confessing all my sins I have collected in the past years, especially in the presence of someone else as a witness, made me shudder. I was terrified, but convinced that it was absolutely necessary for my spiritual progress. It's a lot easier to admit and confess our sins to God in private, but it's a whole other story when we do it when someone else is listening. Somehow, by doing it that way, our sins get exposed and are made more real, while also being released from deep inside of our souls. It's like free therapy. One day I finally gathered enough courage. I came home, got a notebook out and jotted down everything I could remember that I had to release and let go from my broken soul. Wow! What a daunting task! There was a lot!

That first Confession was one of the most difficult things I have ever done in my life.

I told everything I could remember, even the worst stuff that I would tell no one otherwise. At first, I didn't feel like much changed inside, but slowly the hardened bricks of my soul started falling off. I began feeling lighter and more peaceful. I started forgiving myself for the things I was so shamed of. I really felt that God forgave me, and Jesus was right there by my side. Those were the most liberating feelings. I had so much weight lifted off my chest— I was finally able to breathe.

Next step after Confession was to ask for forgiveness from those people who I might have hurt in the past. No one told me to do that, but internally I felt it was necessary. I went ahead and sent a lengthy message to my ex-husband Steve who, I think, I have hurt the most, and asked for forgiveness for all the mean words, all nasty fights, and all the horrible moments that I put him through. I sent another message to my friend who had been through thick and thin with me, but who I also hurt in the past. When I got an almost immediate positive response—that's when I felt truly forgiven. I knew I was on the right track. Things were looking up. I was in a much better mood and smiled all the time. A huge rock fell off my soul.

But there were and ARE still plenty of rocks… *This rocky, rocky road called recovery…*

CHAPTER NINE

Next Stage

A FTER HEARING IN Confession about my failed relationships, Father Gabriel urged me to stay single for at least a year and work on my spiritual life on my own. I agreed, but God had a different plan for me. I stayed single for three months. Before, I was never looking for a serious relationship and didn't have any desire to have children. I was always in some kind of dysfunctional relationship (including two of my previous marriages), but I really didn't think I was cut out to be a wife and mother. Being single was new to me, though. A couple months down the road, I started feeling a little lonely and thought it would be great to finally settle down, get married, and have an actual family. That was a huge change from my old ways of thinking. It was a miracle in itself. However, I didn't think settling down was possible. There were no decent men around. In fact, I didn't even know what a decent man would look like since I didn't have one decent father/man figure in my life.

Until I met Chris...

We met at a New Year's party.

Three months later we did a mud run together in Charleston, SC. Chris was tall, handsome, successful, charming, and oh, so sexy—the captain of our team! I got smitten pretty much right away. I felt small and unimportant next to him, and I definitely never thought he would want to do anything with a broken girl like me. But he did—he liked me too. We went out on our first date to see *God is Not Dead*. We were holding hands and kissed, but he wanted to take things slowly. That was new to me too, and I loved that. I wanted to do something different this time, and I knew I didn't want to screw this one up because I would probably never meet a guy like him. Seeing that movie with him while I was going through my spiritual transformation was certainly symbolic, and I knew it wasn't by mere chance. God was very much alive!

At dinner that evening, as we were talking about my past, and I explained that I was in the process of life recovery, Chris listened carefully and said, "I see something in you. I have a feeling that we should be together." I almost fell off the chair. There was no way that this Prince Charming was sitting in front of me, asking me to be his girlfriend. It was clearly another miracle! I naturally got excited, but was hesitant at the same time. I explained to him I wasn't trying to get into another relationship that was only going to last for a short period. I made it clear that if we decided to go for it, it would be forever and we would work it out no matter what issues arise during our relationship. I finally wanted to be taken seriously. I finally wanted to take someone seriously. Two weeks later, we moved in together. Two days after that, I quit working nights. Chris helped me a lot financially in the beginning, until I was able to get on my own two feet.

Chris fixed and sold my car and helped me to get another one (big deal for Myrtle beach because there is no public transportation). I got my driver's license back and could drive myself to work. My grandmother's apartment in Russia got sold. Mom sent me some money so I could straighten some bills and renew my green card. I felt like a human being again. Being on the bottom, surviving and coming out on the other side of it can't compare with anything I have ever experienced.

Boy, we had fun though! I didn't realize how many friends Chris had. Some of them were our mutual friends, so I had no problem blending in his circle. The problem was—every one of those friends and even his whole family loved to drink! Constant cookouts, restaurants, bars, concerts, nightclubs, and house football parties never ended. Triggers were everywhere. I quickly fell back into old habits. Often we stayed up until sunrise, drinking and talking, and then slept during the day.

Seeing myself going downhill again, I started having doubts whether Chris was the right guy for me. When I wanted to stay home and have a quiet evening, he would choose to invite friends over instead, or go out somewhere. I started going back to church and went to a few more Confessions after which Father Gabriel carefully suggested I should consider going to an AA meeting. Oh, how embarrassing that was for me to hear! He confided in me that there was a parishioner in our church who went to AA, and that if I decided to try it out, she could go with me for support. I cringed at the thought, but took his advice and went anyway.

That first meeting was super awkward. I felt so out of place and didn't know where to look and what to say that when my turn came and I had to introduce myself and say, *"I'm an alcoholic",* I turned bright red and quickly spat it out. It was a hard pill to swallow. No one seemed to pay any attention to my discomfort. Everyone kindly said hi and moved on to the next person. After that first time, it didn't seem like that big of a deal anymore. I slowly started accepting the fact that I had a serious alcohol problem, and so did everyone else in the group. Hearing everyone's stories and being able to share mine without feeling judged felt like a relief. Another brick fell off my soul.

Things got bad with Chris. I decided that our relationship wasn't going anywhere, so I broke up with him. I moved in with the same friend where I first accepted Jesus back into my life. I needed to pray a lot and figure out why I failed again. In the meantime, I missed Chris and didn't want to give up on him completely, but wanted to give us some time to think about our life priorities. For two weeks, I didn't respond to any messages, but he kept trying to connect. I prayed to God to help me resolve the situation according to His will. Realizing I would have to respond to Chris eventually, I went to talk to Father Gabriel. He advised me to invite Chris to talk to him and myself in the church so that we could come to the right decision together. I wasn't sure if Chris would be up for something like that, but to my surprise, he did show up for the meeting with Father Gabriel, who explained to him how much progress I had made in my life recovery before I met Chris. He told Chris I needed more support from him so that I did not fall back into my alcohol abuse cycle. He asked him straight up whether he was ready to do that for me. Chris agreed, and the next stage of our relationship began. I moved back in after two months and we started over.

I went back to AA a few more times. Since I had so much support at my church, I decided I didn't really need AA any longer. I got what I needed from AA (or so I thought), which was the acceptance of the fact that I had a problem and needed help. I just didn't believe that saying I was an alcoholic all the time would actually help me stop being one! I became even more active at my church instead.

I wanted to serve others, so I volunteered at Helping Hand of Myrtle Beach. At first, I was working in the pantry. Later on, I drove the van, picking up food from grocery stores, and gave it out to the poor and homeless, and afterwards, I started processing food stamps and Medicare applications. The Holy Spirit was clearly working in me. I felt elated almost all the time. My faith was stronger than ever. I wanted to help as many people as I could. My heart and my soul were wide open. Once I took in a homeless heroin addict and helped him with food and money. I drove him to Columbia and put him in a rehab. I got a phone call from the police three days later. He left the rehab and was roaming the streets. I woke Chris up in the middle of the night, and we drove for three hours to pick him up. We let him stay at our house for two weeks. We gave him clean clothes, food, and a place to sleep. I drove him around to apply for jobs. I brought him to church. He kept saying he wanted to get better, but I later found him high on heroin again. Eventually we had to let him go, and he ended up taking a bus to Miami. He wasn't ready to get unstuck. The devil was stronger, and he even admitted it. Sad. He didn't want to do the work.

Chris and I got my married two years after we met. It has been almost seven years since we first met. We love each other and support each other no matter what. We traveled to Russia, after 15 years from when I first left, to visit my mom and stepdad, who stayed together and have been married for 20 years now. God worked miracles in their lives, too. Not only they both stopped drinking but also they live comfortably in the two-bedroom apartment that I bought for them, and they recently have bought a small summer cottage outside of the city. Two years after the first visit, we went again, but this time with our little son, Noah, who we had prayed for over a year. Everything lined up for us. We both are financially stable. We bought our first house, which is a huge deal for me, considering where I spent most of my childhood and never having a place of my own. We both have reliable cars. I never thought I would enjoy a normal life. I never had a normal life. People say normal life is boring. Not for me. I had my fun times, and I also had my traumatic times, so I'm totally fine with normal now!

Even though, with God's help, I was able to completely transform my life in every way possible, there is still so much more to recover from. After all, family dysfunction is passed on from generation to generation, and it's not so easy to break it. I talk to mom every other day on the phone, but it's still difficult for me to accept love from her. I really don't think she realizes what her dysfunctional behavior did to me, or even remembers most of the things that I remember, so I am trying to accept that. I understand she was brought up in dysfunction herself and just played out the generational curse with her own life, but right now I'm just in the state of grief over my lost adolescence. Knowing how much I love my son, it's hard for me to understand how she could choose men and alcohol over me. That just shows how messed up and evil the consequences of dysfunction can be. And so many parents do this to their kids without thinking twice about it! I know, as my recovery progresses, I will be able to accept and forgive wholeheartedly, just like God forgave me. Hopefully, one day I will be able to say that I love her because I really want to. I'm grateful to God that my parents are alive, sober, doing well, and pray for us and tell us they love us.

It has been eighteen years since I moved to The US—seven of those years I have been in recovery. Next step for me is to fulfill my purpose. I finally found it. I am listening to God's guidance and sharing my story with all of you hoping it will make a difference in someone's life. It's never too late to be better than you were yesterday! It's never too late to become different from your parents!

Parents!
Please love your children and cherish them!
Find your dysfunction and stop it!
All we want is to be loved and accepted.
Let your kids be happier than you were,
That, in turn, will make YOU happier.
Remember that children don't forget hurt.
They carry it with them their entire lives sometimes.
Do you really want that?
It's not too late to turn it all around!

Love,
K s e n i a   K .

SECTION TWO

15

TAKEAWAYS

*and Practical Steps of Action Towards Life
Recovery and Character Transformation*

*"The great end of life is not
knowledge but action."*

–THOMAS HENRY HUXLEY

1

Admitting you can't do it any longer and something has to change.

"Don't be a product of your circumstances,
be a product of your decisions."

— ANONYMOUS

First and the most important step towards any kind of recovery is the acknowledgment that you need it. Desire to change can start by lurking somewhere in the back of your mind, amid all the chaos that your life has become. The more and the longer you mess up, the harder it will be to get started—the longer your road to recovery might be. Ideally, take the first steps as soon as you have a glimpse of clarity. In reality, though, most of us wait till we hit our lowest point—our rock bottom.

Why is that? Do we want to see how far we can make it without changing and still be able to survive? Or is it because we challenge God to find out how much patience He has? Or is it because we don't believe that we can change anything anyway, so we continue living in the victim mentality? What are we trying to prove and to who? Most likely, we are not trying to prove anything—we are just numb and broken and don't have motivation and energy to collect our broken pieces and start gluing them together. We don't know what a normal life looks like, and we are not confident that we will even be *able* to have a normal life. So we keep working on our self-destruction.

Admitting we have a problem is difficult. Admitting feels like defeat. Admitting is embarrassing—except we don't think about all the embarrassing stuff we have done because of our problem. Admitting we have a problem and desire to change go hand in hand. If you desire to change, but are too proud to admit the problem, it's very unlikely that you will be successful in your journey to recovery. Your pride will be in your way. Pride might prevent you from asking and accepting help from others, from working on your own character flaws, instead of playing a victim and blaming others in your unfortunate circumstances, but the most important of all—pride will prevent you from asking God for help. We are all proud people. We want to feel important. We want to feel in charge and in control. Look at what you have done to yourself? Does it look like you were an outstanding leader for yourself? If you are reading this book and you are the one in need of recovery, then the answer is most likely NO.

You don't have to admit your struggle to anyone else yet, but first to yourself, and then God. Being in denial led you to where you are now—lost, hopeless, and confused. You are asking yourself, *how in the world did I get here? Is this the life I was meant to live and die like an unknown, invisible insect?* If you are asking these types of questions, you are already starting in the right direction. The beginning is the most difficult. You will have to change the way you think, the way you act, and the way you relate to people and situations around you.

> *"People who are unhappy and who live "broken lives" have often been without the results they desire for so long that they no longer believe they can produce the results that they want. They do little or nothing to tap their potential and begin to try to find out how they can get their life to where they're doing as little as possible."*
>
> **—TONY ROBBINS**

2

Pray for God's help (even if you don't really believe in it yet).

"Lord, I believe; help my unbelief!"

(Mark 9:24)

We should pray ceaselessly, but it's not as easy for some people as it is for others. They say, when you pray from the heart, the Holy Spirit Itself prays within you, with you, and through you. First prayer that is necessary when you begin your recovery journey is a simple prayer, where you ask God to come into your life and help you in your recovery. If you don't believe yet, pray anyway and ask God to help your unbelief, like I did.

The Bible teaches us the **Lord's Prayer**:

Our Father, who are in Heaven,
Hallowed be Your name,
Your Kingdom come.
Your will be done on earth
as it is in Heaven.
Give us this day Our Daily Bread,
And forgive us our trespasses as we forgive
those who trespass against us,
And lead us not into temptation,
but deliver us from evil.

This is not the only way to pray. Any prayer that comes from your heart is good. I often use prayer books because I have a hard time finding the right words. Prayer books are compilations of prayers by other people. There are a lot of wonderful, deep prayers that I, on my own, would have never come up with to express how I feel. These prayers can be adjusted to the situation you are in. Even though it's best to pray from the heart, I firmly believe that it's better to pray, even if you are not really feeling up to it, rather than not to pray at all. God knows our struggle. Sometimes your attention will wander while praying, but the Holy Spirit can stir up within you when the right word or phrase comes along during the prayer. As long as God sees your efforts to have a relationship with Him, He will open your heart to prayer.

Try your best to make prayer a habit. For example, schedule some time first thing in the morning and some time before bed, if possible. If it's not doable, you can pray anytime. It's better to do it alone, behind closed doors, but it's also great to pray with your family, friends, or anyone who is willing to do it with you. Prayer is powerful any day, anytime, anywhere. If it is uncomfortable and even feels a little weird at first, don't worry, it happens to everyone. With time and genuine effort, it will become easier and eventually become your second nature. You will start needing prayer. You might feel uncomfortable to go about your day without having prayed, so you can say a quick prayer, *Lord, Jesus Christ, Son of God, be merciful to me, or Sinner.* Or simply, *Lord, have mercy!*

Sometimes I struggle with prayer; sometimes it comes to me easily. Sometimes I just don't have the energy and praying seems like a lot of work; sometimes I feel a strong call to prayer. I feel guilty when I don't get myself to pray, but God knows my weakness. He knows I want to pray, so maybe on those days I should just ask him to forgive me. He knows what we need either way. He knows desires of our hearts.

> *"Beliefs are the compass and maps that guide us… Without beliefs or the ability to tap into them, people… are like a motorboat without a motor or rudder."*
>
> **—TONY ROBBINS**

3

Don't do it alone!
Look for help and
support from others.

"But woe to him who is alone when he falls."

(ECCLESIASTES 4:10)

Man was never meant to be alone. Having a friend by your side who accepts you the way you are and can support you on your path to change is extremely powerful. They say misery loves company. That is absolutely true, but I firmly believe that joy loves company too. Sharing the joy of even the smallest progress in the right direction with a trusted friend can be a great motivator. When someone is genuinely happy and excited for you, especially when you are in the beginning of your recovery journey, it serves as reassurance that you made the right choice. A trusted friend can be someone you were friends with in the past, but cut communication off because he or she did not fit your dysfunctional lifestyle at the time; it can be your husband or partner, who had been waiting for you to get clean; it can even be your child (depending on the age). In either case, the first thing to do is to be completely honest with them and ask for forgiveness if you hurt them in any way by your unruly behavior. Another option can be a pastor from a local church who knows about your situation and is eager to support you on your journey (like in my case), or you can join an AA group (or similar support group) and get a sponsor who had been through the recovery journey, or it can even be one of your bar-fly friends, but only if they seriously want to change as well. Here, though, you have to be extra careful, because the temptation to relapse can be a lot stronger. Both of you will have to have more mature support, someone who is not a freshman, just coming out of the bar.

There are various support groups available whether you want to recover from alcohol, drug, food, sex addiction, gambling, shopping, and even co-dependency. Examples of these are Celebrate Recovery (CR), Alcoholics Anonymous (AA), Adult Children of Alcoholics (ACA), Sexaholics Anonymous (SA), or any local support groups. Usually those are in-person meet ups, but during COVID many of them moved to Zoom and phone meetings, or online chats. What's good about them is that these groups are filled with people just like you—people who came to realize that their lives became unruly, and they need help to make serious, meaningful changes for the sake of their families, but first and foremost—for themselves. Besides, there are always more mature recovered people who can support you every step of the way. You will meet new people and make new friends, who might become your lifetime friends. Having so much support and being able to share your wins and failures without being judged is exhilarating and extremely motivating. These people will push you to keep going, even in your most difficult moments.

The more support you have, the easier your transition to the new, transformed life will be. If you have a trusted childhood friend, family member, pastor, and you are a part of a support group, the chances that you will reach your goal are so much higher. Now, if you, at one point, decide that it is too difficult and you give up, it does not matter how much support you have. It simply won't work!

A word of warning though: try not to jump from being addicted to alcohol, drugs, sex, or whatever, to getting addicted to your support group. You can become what they call a "dry drunk". That's when you stay physically sober, but you change little about your behavior. Support groups are a great way to start, and it's definitely a good idea to go through a 12-step program. Going to meetings and connecting with people will certainly aid in staying physically sober, especially in the very beginning when you are still weak, but I personally don't think that meetings should be the only method to use in recovery.

My main advice is to try to figure out why you turn to self-destructive behaviors in the first place.

Is it because you don't like yourself sober? Lack of self-worth? Social anxiety? Do you think people won't accept you the way you really are? Fear of abandonment and rejection? Lack of courage to face your fears? What is at the core of your addiction? Is it childhood trauma that makes you depressed? Finding the real reason helped me to finally kick the habit and work on my ultimate healing.

There are tons of resources to help answer your questions: books, Internet, YouTube videos, therapy. We live in the information age, so if you really want to dig deep, you will find the answers. I also recommend going back to your first memory as a child and write out everything that you remember from that moment and up that might have affected you, good and bad, and see what comes up from your memory. Addictions and bad habits help us repress our bad memories, feelings, and emotions, but if we don't release them, there will most likely be no ultimate healing, because trauma is stored in our bodies, that, in turn, affects our physiology and psychology in many unhealthy ways. There is a ton of information out there on how to release the stored trauma from your body. I don't think there is one right way. Experiment and find what works for you. Some childhood trauma (bad sexual abuse by your father, for example) can be too painful to bring back up, and it can put you in a state of deep depression. Look for professional help if you think you need it!

4

Hope and do what God says.

"He who has ears let him hear".

(MATTHEW 11:15)

Having hope and expecting that you will succeed in your recovery journey is paramount to your progress. Most likely, you will have self-doubt throughout your journey. Without hope, there is almost no point in even starting the recovery process. First, it is necessary to ask God for help, and hope and expect that He will come through. Even though the help might not come right away, it's important to start taking steps of your own in the right direction. If you don't have a Bible, get one! There is no better guide to live than the Bible itself, especially if self-discipline is what you need, and trust me, you need it! Besides being a guide on how to behave properly, the Bible provides hope, assurance that God loves you and that you are forgiven, if you genuinely repent, besides many other things. If you are not a Christian, or you were baptized in the past and lost your faith, or never really understood it to begin with, you will find a great wisdom that will touch your heart and mind, as long as you are willing to be open-minded.

The Bible is not an easy read, that's for sure. When you first start, you might read just a few verses or a page and have an urge to put it down. The evil one hates it! Take as much time as you need to get familiar with different sections of the Bible. Don't lose hope and stop. God will speak to you through His Word, I can assure you of that. You will know when that happens, because you will notice that the way you think will begin to change. Give it time and be patient (I know we want everything to happen right now, right?!).

Bible studies are a great way to get involved in learning about faith. In a group setting, you will ask questions and get answers to the most difficult and confusing parts of the Bible. Have an open mind and be eager to learn, even if you don't initially agree with some things you read or hear. For me, it wasn't a one-day process, but an ongoing, never-ending one, because every time I read the Bible, I learn something new—God reveals more and more mysteries to me. If you need more help to figure out what certain Bible passages say, you can always ask for clarification from people who are more mature in their Christian faith and more experienced in their walk with God. Prayer is the one thing that must be practiced for the rest of your life. Especially in the beginning, when you first start your walk with God. For me, it's easier if I learn the prayer that speaks to me instead of making one up, unless it's something specific that I need or simply thank God for. If you don't fully believe yet, admit it and ask God to help your unbelief. If your desire to know God is genuine, eventually, He will respond, and you will know when it happens. "Ask, and it shall be given you; seek, and ye shall find; knock, and it shall be opened to you." (Matthew 7:7)

Don't give up!

5

Remove yourself from the situation.

"It's OK to be scared."

—ANONYMOUS

If you find yourself in a situation toxic to you, it is necessary to find any way possible to remove yourself from it. Examples could be a toxic relationship, where your partner is an abusive alcoholic or drug user, or if you work at a bar or club where alcohol/ drugs are all around you (like in my case). Being in a toxic environment will make it a lot more difficult to stay away from your unhealthy habit. Even though it might be impossible to get out of the toxic environment right away, start looking for opportunities and solutions as soon as you can.

Facebook or any social media outlet can be a dangerous place if it connects you with the people you used to party with. Consider deleting your social media accounts or taking a break while you are getting better, or create a new page where you only add people who can be beneficial and supportive of your journey. Working with the same people with whom you used to go out for a drink after work, will not only serve as a trigger but also might raise many questions by those people. They might start asking you why you don't go out with them anymore. If you try to explain to people who don't think you have a problem and don't take your desire to stop drinking seriously why you decided to change suddenly, they might laugh at you, think you are being weird, and either try to seduce you back into their circle, or start talking behind your back, which makes the work environment uncomfortable. If quitting your job is not an option, do your best to reduce the time you spend with the trigger people and keep your progress to yourself. When you become mentally, spiritually, and physically stronger, and people at your work start seeing real positive changes, then you can start opening up and possibly encourage your coworkers to change their ways as well.

I can't stress enough how important it is to remove yourself from ALL possible toxic relationships. It can be a family member, like your mother, father, or sibling, friend, or your spouse, lover, or domestic partner; if you're older, it can even be your son or daughter. The people who are the closest to you tend to have the most influence on your mental state. They are the ones who know you the most and can push the right buttons, control and manipulate you, which will absolutely hinder your progress. Sad to say, but the ones who are closest to us hurt us the most because we are emotionally attached to them.

If you are in a relationship with another alcoholic or drug user who is not willing to change with you, it is better to leave the relationship as soon as it becomes possible. As scary as it sounds at first, it will probably be one of the most life-changing steps. If all you're experiencing is hurt and suffering, whether it is mental, emotional, physical, or all three, there is no reason to stay in the relationship. Even if you love that person, it will do you and him/her good, if at least one of you gets on the right path. They might realize that they, too, want to change only after they see you leave and understand there's nobody there to support their own habits and addictions. If you have friends who are enabling you in your bad habits, you will have to either let them go, if they are not supportive, and only see them again when you are strong enough and you know for sure that you won't be sucked back in. Most of the time, those kinds of friends just need company and can not care less about your actual needs, which are sobriety, stability, self-acceptance, confidence, love, and peace of mind, besides other needs. If your friends are supportive of your change, by all means, stay connected and check on them, but still remove yourself from triggering situations like parties and cookouts. You might even have to miss a few birthdays!

6

Instead of complaining and blaming everyone else and your circumstances, look for solutions.

"Face your life, it's pain, its pleasure, leave no path untaken."

—Neil Gaiman

Yes, sometimes life, so to speak, can beat you on the head. But you are the one who makes a choice of how to react to those situations and circumstances. A bad habit or addiction does not become a habit or addiction in one day. It starts slowly; your body and your mind become more tolerant and, gradually, you need more and more of what you think makes you feel better. Losing a loved one, childhood trauma, stressful job, or a devastating relationship, can leave you depressed, lost, insecure, and not sure how to continue living.

There is a process of grief that you will have to go through, but if there are no supportive people around you, the grief process can lead you into the abyss of misery, and it's very easy to slip into self-destructive behaviors. In certain situations, you will need a combination of supportive friends and family, support groups and/or church, and professional help. It seems like a lot of work. It makes it so much easier to stuff yourself with unhealthy food, drink alcohol, or do drugs instead—to numb the soul-excruciating pain. Whatever you decide to choose, it is still your own choice. Don't blame others, unfortunate circumstances, and especially God for your own choices. I won't sugarcoat it for you—your choices led you to where you are today! God gave us free will, so we take part in our own destiny. There are choices that will lead us to life, and there are choices that will lead us to death—spiritual, mental, or even physical.

As much as I wanted to blame alcohol for my mom's actions and always tried to find an excuse for her behavior, **she** was the one who made a choice to pick up the bottle each time and emotionally abandon me, instead of dealing with her issues and find ways to resolve them. As much as I want to blame alcohol for my own behaviors, **I** was the one who made a choice to numb myself and act out. No one **made** me do it! Unfortunately, Russia is known for alcoholism. That curse has been passed on from generation to generation for ages, and most people probably don't even think that there should or **can** be something done about it. Also, in the past there were not that many help resources available. These days, when resources are everywhere, and a lot of them are free, there is no excuse not to find a solution and break the curse of dysfunction (whether it's alcohol, food, marijuana, sex, or something else).

Even though other people might have caused a lot of your misfortunes or trauma, blaming them and constantly complaining will not make any difference. Vice versa, you will keep dwelling on the past and relieving your hurt and suffering. It's okay to confide in a trusted person, or a therapist, or your pastor, but after that—it's time to ask for help. Get out of the victim mentality and start looking for solutions. Blaming God is even worse.

Accept everything the way it is, pray, ask for help, and act.

> *"You take your life in your own hands, and what happens? A terrible thing: no one to blame."*
>
> —ERICA JONG

7

Identify and avoid your triggers.

"The one who removes the mountain begins by carrying away small stones."

—**A**NONYMOUS

In order to know what triggers your bad habits/ addictions, you need to identify all your triggers. You can do it by noticing when you get an urge and, preferably, writing it down. Some obvious triggers for an alcoholic are being in a bar or liquor section in the grocery store, being around family members who drink, or having beers in your fridge. Some more subtle ones are getting upset at something or someone, being stressed, leaving work after a long day, or going to a social gathering. The more observant you become of your everyday activities and the feelings they evoke, the more aware you will become of your triggers. A good idea is to avoid the most obvious triggers first and, as you are more aware of the more subtle ones, it will surprise you how many triggers you will find once you start monitoring your thoughts and feelings closely. For example, you might notice that, when you get home after work, you feel tired and immediately open a bottle of beer or pour yourself a glass of wine so that you can mentally relax before you even get to eat dinner. Most of these are just habits and can be re-programmed.

Once you identify your triggers, it's time to reduce, avoid them altogether, or replace those activities that cause the unhealthy urge with something more healthy, productive, spiritual, or creative. They say *an idle mind is the devil's playground*. That's very true, especially for those of you struggling with an addiction. If you are used to binge-watching Netflix with a case of beer every night after work, you might want to replace this activity by visiting an evening service at a church or going to an AA meeting. If you don't feel like going anywhere, move to a room with no TV, open your Bible, or read a Christian book (or any book you really like), pray, watch a sermon if you are not a reader, learn something, organize or clean, go for a walk, take a bike ride, or work on a craft. Keep yourself busy and most important of all, pray every time you have an unhealthy urge until it disappears. Purge your immediate environment from everything that is unhealthy, causes negative feelings, and triggers your habit. Remove alcohol and/or drugs from the house (alcoholism/drug addiction), clean your fridge and pantry from unhealthy foods (food addiction), give away your game console to a friend (video game addiction), and so on. Instead, fill your house with positive, healthy things. The more time you spend doing things that please God, the more you will fill your mind with the right thoughts and emotions. None of this means you won't have a relapse, but when and if you do, pick yourself back up, analyze what exactly happened and what urged you to relapse, start over, but do something different this time. I'm not saying you should give yourself permission to relapse and not take it seriously, but what I am saying is it can certainly happen.

Once again, I know it all sounds like a lot of work, because it is, and yes, you will have to put a lot of effort and take **part in your own deliverance**— sitting on the couch and expect good things to happen to you won't work, even though God is all powerful, and it is possible that He can cleanse your mind all at once (which wasn't my case).

> *"The pain of discipline is a lot easier to handle than the pain of regret... Action is what produces results."*
>
> **—ANONYMOUS**

8

A special note about church

Okay, so you can find God anywhere, but being around like-minded Christians, whether they are more mature or just starting out on their own faith journey, can make your recovery so much easier, so much more joyful, and so much more meaningful! Finding the right church, where you feel comfortable and accepted, is very important. I love my Orthodox Church, that is very traditional, but I understand everyone is different, and God can show up anywhere, as long as your desire to know Him is genuine. I will be more than happy to talk to you about Orthodox Christian faith anytime, but this book is not about that specifically.

I prefer a quiet church where I can stand or sit in silence and contemplate on what is being read, said, and sung. To me, being in my church is sort of escape (healthy escape this time) from the cares of the rest of the world. Music, chanting, glowing of the candles, beauty of the church decor, people standing silently and reverently put me in the right mood and bring the feelings of peace to my soul. I have visited other churches and heard wonderful sermons, but I stay loyal to my church because it is literally like my home. The Orthodox Church is a traditional one. We are encouraged to fast on certain days, wear non-revealing clothes, go to Confession, and take Communion. I personally love the traditions of the church—they add more depth to personal prayer and worshipping at home. Transitioning from wild party life with no rules, I certainly needed some structure and lots of discipline; following the traditions of the church helped me get my head straight, develop respect, and start losing my pride, and oh, I had a lot of that, and it is still work in progress!

Now, this kind of structure and discipline might scare some people, even though I firmly believe that's exactly what we need in the beginning, at least until we develop self-discipline, and you might choose to go to a church with live band music and listen to an effective preacher. This usually evokes strong feelings that lay dormant inside of the person, and maybe that's exactly what he or she needs at the moment. Not all churches are equal. If you don't like one, go to another one, and keep looking until you find the one where you feel comfortable. Your primary goal is to develop a personal relationship with God, after all. Immerse yourself in the Word of God. Surround yourself with devoted, genuine, godly people. Have a burning desire for God. He will open your heart, and He **will** heal you.

Do be careful though. Before committing yourself to a church, make sure that the chosen church teaches nothing that deviates from the Word of God. There are multiple denominations and even more interpretations, so it's easy to get lost. In the Orthodox Church, I know I don't have to worry about that because its traditions and teachings can be traced all the way back to the times of the Apostles.

"Replace fear with unwavering faith."
— HAL ELROD

9

Lower your expectations. Strive to please God.

"... Walk worthy of the Lord, fully pleasing Him, being fruitful in every good work and increasing in the knowledge of God..."

(COLOSSIANS 1:10)

Setting high expectations for yourself right away can lead to disappointment and failure. Don't assume that you will get rid of your addiction the moment you decide to make a change, or the minute you pray (even though I personally know people who experienced that!), or as soon as you step into an AA building. Even though God can show a miracle and remove your desire for the unwanted substance or activity once and for all, for most of us, it's just the beginning of a long journey, the rocky road, full of self-discoveries, joy, and disappointments. It's good to set a goal—to quit drinking for good, for example, but it's okay to start with small steps and measure progress as you go. You will see what works and what doesn't, what triggers you and what's not affecting you too much, what needs a lot of work and what needs just a slight adjustment. Examples of small steps can be avoiding drinking shots and having only light beer instead, having a drink only on the weekends, and skip the rest of the week. Not everyone can physically stop all alcohol at once. Cutting down is not a bad idea. Now, if you notice that instead of your usual shot you end up drinking a twelve pack of beer, it's time to reconsider whether you are on the right track.

Measure your success by progress, not the end result. Take small steps every day and celebrate (not with another glass of beer) small wins. There are going to be good days, and there are going to be bad days, when you feel like giving up. Expect ups and downs. After all, you are still weak and have a long way to build character strength and powerful will. Don't beat yourself up. Don't drown in guilt if you fall back in the habit once in a while. Be remorseful, but don't dwell on the failure. Lower your expectations, but have high hopes, and believe that God is working with you and in you. Don't expect too much of yourself, but do expect God's help. If you fall once, get back up, acknowledge where you went in the wrong direction, identify the triggers, confess your failures, shake it off, and move on. Every day is a new day. Every day is a blessing and fresh start.

If you feel you are slipping back into old habits too often, reach out for support. Call or visit someone you trust who can pray with you and give you support and guidance. Don't be too proud or ashamed of your fall. We are all human. We make mistakes. We are not perfect. We are vulnerable. "For when I am weak, then I am strong." (Corinthians 12:10) Anytime you feel challenged, pray. God hears our prayers. He is with us always. He knows our hearts, and He knows our minds.

Set your eyes and mind on pleasing God, instead of focusing on your failures. Spiritual warfare is real. It is lifelong. As long as God sees your genuine efforts to change, He will be there to hold you by your hand and lead you to a new life.

Eventually, you will have to kick the habit for good.

Keep your head up!

10

Thank God for being alive.

> *"Although no one can go back and make*
> *a brand new start, anyone can start from*
> *now and make a brand new ending."*
>
> —C ARL B ARD

No, really, thank God for being alive. Not everyone makes it. Too many lives that could be saved end; some—with no remembrance by anyone at all; some—grieved by the loved ones who stayed to live; some—remembered with anger and resentment. Thank God you are alive and still have a chance to change everything. Start thinking back to your addiction history. Remember all the times God spared you. I don't believe in pure chances or coincidences. You could end up driving drunk and killing yourself or someone else, whether it be a child in the back of someone's car, an elderly person, slowly trying to cross the street while you were flying and swerving on the road, or a pregnant woman. It could be anyone. Instead, you were arrested, got a DUI, and no one got killed.

What else could have happened?

You could have had alcohol poisoning anytime you drank too much. You could be drugged in a club. You could be raped and wouldn't even remember it. You could black out and hurt someone. You could lose your job, your house, your children. The list goes on and on. Be thankful none of that happened. Or maybe some of it did, but you are still here, and you have a chance to fix it. Start being thankful for everything. God loves a grateful heart. Start thanking God for every small progress, every little win, even if it's seemingly unimportant, but you know it matters to you.

Start being grateful for all the relationships you were able to keep. Be thankful for and to all the people who have stuck with you through thick and thin. Wake up each day and thank God for having a chance to start fresh that day, even if you messed up again. Thank God for being able to still have a sound mind to be able to read His Word and comprehend what is being said. Be grateful for still having clothes on your shoulders and a place to live. If you lost everything, be grateful for the desire and willingness to change.

Pray for being able to hear God's voice and thank Him when you do.

Pray for being able to meet the right people who can support you on your journey to life recovery— thank God when you do.

Pray for the health of your body and mind so you can take the right action and do God's work.

Thank Him for waking you up. Thank Him for all the lessons you learned.

Thank Him for all the trials He allowed you to have to finally come to Him for help.

He needs you just as much as you need Him. You are just as valuable as anyone else. He sent His own Son to save people like you and me.

> ### *Thank God for everything!*

11

Follow through on your commitments.

Think back to the period when all you did was party and sleep, and maybe work sometimes. You will remember making promises to people and not following through—empty promises. For example, you told your kids you would spend an entire day with them, but ended up sleeping all day because you were too hungover to get up. You might have promised your spouse to go see a specialist and ask for help but instead, you kept driving to the bar after work and stayed out late. You could have promised your elderly parents to come visit and never did—you came up with all kinds of excuses for why you couldn't come again—you were too embarrassed to show them what you had become. You could have promised your best friend to go out for lunch and talk about good old days like you used to, but lunchtime was too early for you to be out and about. And so it went—people lost trust in you.

NOW is the time to follow up on your commitments. NOW is the time to build your trust back. It might take time, but it's a must if you want to progress in your recovery. Relationships are important. They say *actions speak louder than words*; only when people see that you follow through on what you promised, they will start opening up to building a trusting relationship with you again. *Only then* actual change can take place around you. Anyone who loves you will see the difference in your behavior, and they will be eager to support you. Hearts, full of anger, sorrow, and hurt, will start melting.

When you find your church and meet new people, make new friends and meet outside the church to make more personal connections. When you do make a commitment to meet somewhere, show up! Also, make sure to take a shower, wear clean clothes and brush your teeth and hair (if you have access to running water, because not everyone does!). Go to church regularly. The more you immerse yourself in the atmosphere of godliness, the more likely you will learn a lot more and a lot faster about your faith and change your behavior and the way of thinking, accordingly. You are a combination of what and who you surround yourself with. Being around godly people is contagious, believe me!

When you join groups like Celebrate Recovery, Alcoholics Anonymous, and Adult Children of Alcoholics/Dysfunctional families, commit yourself to go to regular meetings. If you have a sponsor, make it a priority to make a plan to meet and discuss your progress and anything that hinders it. When people see how committed you are, they will be more willing to help and support you.

Treat people how you want to be treated.

12

Ask for forgiveness.

Look around you. How many loyal people do you have in your life right now! Is your family still with you? What about your friends? Coworkers? People you used to go to school with? Or is there almost no one left? You might still have your family and friends around. They stayed loyal and supportive, hoping that one day you would get better and things become normal. Does that mean that your relationship with them is as close and warm as it should be? Do you think there is something that is hindering you from having the best relationship with them? During our party lives, we tend to lose our focus on the most important—relationships with the people we love. We tend to be self-centered and prideful. We don't want to be home taking care of dishes, cleaning the house, or teaching our kids responsibility. That's too much work. It's stressful. So we go out to meet our bar friends, and life suddenly seems fun and exciting. We neglect our everyday duties to our spouses, children, and friends, and anyone who is supposed to matter to us.

Finally, people realize they are not on our priority list. They see that we prefer to be everywhere else but with them. It hurts. It brings sadness. Then it grows into anger, resentment, and loss of trust. You might come home wasted and make a scene regularly. You might yell and cuss at your wife when she tries to talk sense into you. You might even hit her. You might even do all that in front of your kids. Or maybe you hit your kids too! Or you are one of those drunks who come home and go to bed, and your family doesn't see you till the next day, when you're hungover and have no energy to spend any time with them or communicate. Day after day, night after night, you are absent. You abandoned your family. Do you have any idea how it affects your loved ones in those moments? Do you realize how much it affects them later in life? Read my story and you will find out.

NOW is the time for you to sit down and think of everyone you might have hurt by your behavior. NOW is the time to lie down your pride and ask for forgiveness—one by one. If you cannot see someone in person, call him or her, or at least send a message. It is one of the most difficult things to do, and your heart will jump out of your chest, but you must ask for forgiveness. Expect different responses. There will be people who will gladly accept your genuine (it has to be genuine) apology; there are going to be those who will get emotional and need time to digest, but will come around later; there might be those who will let out all the hurt and anger that they could not express before because you were not open to listen; there might be those who will be suspicious, or even reject you. Allow them to express their feelings—they deserve to be heard.

Asking for forgiveness and fixing your broken relationships piece by piece is groundbreaking. It is as absolutely necessary for *your* healing, as for those who were hurt *by you*.

What a great feeling of relief when someone says, "I forgive you!"

13

A special note about Confession.

"Confess your trespasses to one another and pray for one another, that you may be healed"

(JAMES 5:16)

Knowing yourself takes time and effort, and it will take much humility to face all your wrongdoings. It is hard to do it just in private with yourself, but it is significantly harder to confess to someone else, whether it is your family, friend, or priest. Whatever you choose to do, do not confess to the wrong person! If you open up to a family member or friend, make sure they are the ones who will not judge you, but are ready to listen and provide support in every way possible. If you confess in front of the priest, like I did and still do, make sure you get to know him first and have some heart to heart talks before you give it all away. There's nothing worse than making a heartfelt confession and be betrayed by someone.

The difference between confessing to God in private and opening up to someone else is—it takes getting down from your high horse of pride and making it more real, coming out in the open when someone else is listening to you. It is a lot easier to confess to God in private; plus, God already knows everything about you, anyway. By doing it only in private, we deprive ourselves from letting our sins out of our heart and mind. There is something powerful in confessing to another. I personally prefer confessing to my spiritual father at my church. I know I don't have to hold anything back, and he always gives me great spiritual advice. I have had a wonderful experience with my Confessions; I feel something is not right when I miss too many weeks of Confession; things pile up in my mind and in my heart.

Confession is not a onetime thing. The first one is the longest and most difficult, but afterwards it is a sort of maintenance confession; as humans, we tend to make mistakes all the time, so there is always room to improve. Regular confession gives you an opportunity to make a clearing of your sins the way of life, not just a onetime event.

It is understandable that it can be very uncomfortable to open up to another human being at first, and that is totally normal; it took me awhile in the beginning. After a few times it gets easier, unless you screwed up really badly and are extremely ashamed of yourself again. When you experience guilt and shame, remember that you are focusing on yourself too much. Instead, focus on God and confess your wrongdoing. Next—start over! It is a good idea to write out everything that comes to mind when you do your first self-inventory. This way, your mind is not all over the place. Some things might come up that you might have forgotten about or simply didn't think were that important. First time doing it is very emotional and nerve-racking, especially when you confess in front of someone else. Confess to God alone first. Confess to someone else, when and if you feel up to it. God will show you the way. Just make sure you burn your confession notes (so no one can read it and throw back in your face), forgive yourself, believe that He has forgiven you, and don't dwell on any of it any longer, if you can.

14

God's miracles— Synchronicities.

God is truly a miracle worker! Once you pray and ask Him for help, He will start showing Himself here and there. If you listen carefully, you will hear and see things through which God will manifest Himself. Some people call it pure coincidence. I like calling these moments and events synchronicities. You will start noticing the right people showing up or hear things you have been curious about. Someone might invite you to a group where you will find answers to some questions you have. You might run into someone from the past who will have a solution for a problem you have. Someone might mention a good therapist you will be interested to see to deal with some of your deeper issues.

God will deliver what you need for your healing. Your task is to listen and watch, and when you have a clarity moment, follow God's direction, be obedient, and take action. If you are not sure what the right action is, pray about it, and the right answer will come sooner or later. Be patient and don't expect everything to get better right away, even though for me, things were happening quickly. If your heart tells you to help someone else in need, do it. Follow those heart movements. You will recognize God's voice when he speaks to you in your heart.

Take every opportunity to learn something new and useful. Meet new people and make friends. You never know what good can come out of it. Try things out. If something doesn't work, move on and try something different. For example, if the AA meetings are not comfortable for you, try Celebrate Recovery instead, or ACA, or find another group. Don't get upset if something doesn't feel right. If sent by God, it will feel right. Make a note on the things that feel right and continue to explore them. The road to recovery is rocky, but it's also wonderful, full of miracles, and pure joy that you have never experienced before. It will feel like you got a second chance in life and you are the co-creator of that new life—together with God Himself!

When you start seeing progress and results, it will motivate you to keep going. The joy you will experience will bring the feeling of elation and uplift. You will have a natural desire to please God more and more. You will start changing your old ways of thinking and behaving, and you will come to more and more realizations of how unnatural your life was before. You will think that being normal is okay. Being normal is not boring. You will start craving stability. You will be on the right track.

God is all-powerful. "You can do anything through Christ, who strengthens you." (Philippians 4:13) If that were not true, there would not be so many testimonies all over the world. We can't be all crazy. Because God is real and we got to know him, we are here today, finally living a life that has meaning!

"The struggle is part of the story."

—ANONYMOUS

15

Learn and grow!

The biggest issue that I had with Alcoholics Anonymous was saying, *"I'm an alcoholic",* at every meeting.

Honestly, I thought it was important for me to finally admit and accept the fact that I had serious issues with alcohol, but I didn't want to settle for identifying myself as an alcoholic for the rest of my life. When we make *I am* statements, we attach them to our essence, our core—our identity. In my honest opinion, if you continue saying *I am an alcoholic, I am a drug addict, I am a food addict,* and so on, you will continue identifying yourself with it and act like one, and it is not very helpful because you will keep dwelling in that mentality and not move past that much.

They say that alcoholism is incurable, but I don't personally agree. If you figure out why you turn to your vice in certain situations, or when you feel a certain way, what you need to do is work on that specific finding, reprogram it, and keep moving forward. If it's a childhood trauma that you never dealt with, it's necessary to find ways to finally deal with it instead of suppressing the trauma even further. If it's fear of rejection, look back and figure out when you first started having that fear and deal with that particular issue. If you are a people pleaser, find out if it's low self-worth that you need to work on. If it's anger, what is it really that triggers you, and so on. Whatever it is, most likely there is a solution, and in many cases, you might have to get professional help.

You might use a combination of church, prayer, psychotherapy, journaling, reading, Neuro-Linguistic programming (NLP), or even self-hypnosis, if you wish. Our brain is complex, but very powerful organ with amazing abilities, and new, better neural pathways can be formed to replace the old ones, unlike what I was taught when I was in school. Look up discoveries on neuroplasticity and learn for yourself. I'm not a scientist, doctor, or psychologist, but I do read every day, and I learn alternative methods that can help me figure out various aspects of my recovery. I try different things and find what works for me and what doesn't. All of these are great tools that can be used for different things, but remember—only God can truly heal you!

Don't stop learning!

I wish you healing and success in your life recovery journey!

You are definitely worth it!

AFTERWORD

ORIGINALLY, I NAMED this book *Unstuck: Trust God, but Do Your Part...*

One day, as I was in the process of writing one of the last chapters, I realized I was not unstuck—I was still work in progress. There was little progress, actually, because I continued doing the same thing repeatedly; I continued drinking occasionally, depending on the event or situation, and continued feeling guilt and remorse afterwards. I felt distant from God and never seemed truly content. I finally figured out why I felt the way I felt.

Before, I never truly desired to quit alcohol completely. I held on to it because it was something to go to when almost any emotion arose. I was not used to not suppressing feelings and emotions immediately, as they came up, so I kept the habit, just in case. I got my life under control and had a great transformation of character, but I didn't reach the end goal until recently. I got stuck in the limbo, so to speak. I thought it was okay to have a drink or two or more here and there, in good company, or it was okay to go out to dinner with my husband and share a bottle of wine on our anniversary. I thought it was okay to have a big party for my birthday and go out with my girlfriends, get wasted, and feel like a complete piece of garbage the next day. Almost every time I did, though, I felt inadequate. It would usually take me three days to recover and feel more or less normal. I would lie in bed all day after a night out, nauseous, with an excruciating migraine; suffering and feeling guilty, thinking, *Why in the world did I do this to myself again? Why do I still so easily give in to alcohol, especially when I'm stressed or anxious, or have something to celebrate, or looking to having a good time?*

The thing is, these occasions did not happen daily, not even every other day, but only once in a blue moon. I would still beat myself up about it, while everyone else would laugh and tell me how much fun it was. Maybe it was fun for others, but it surely was not fun for me, like it used to be when I first started partying. I'm not twenty years old anymore! I'm a mother of an amazing little boy. I'm a wife. I'm a Christian. This behavior is not appropriate for me any longer, especially after what alcohol did to me and my parents, and their parents.

During my life recovery journey, I never really asked God to remove the desire to drink completely. For some reason, I didn't think it was necessary. Somehow I wanted to hang on to it. The longer I did, though, the more discontent I became. I felt something was missing in my life. I was cold and numb. Finally, as I was writing and telling my reader how to recover from his/her addiction, it came to me that I, myself, am still in need for further recovery. God opened my eyes and put in my heart to pray for complete disappearance of the desire to drink. All the steps I described in my book I had to repeat, but with the end goal in mind this time. I didn't want my son to grow up in the family that praises alcohol. I never want him to see me drunk. I never want to let him down. It's up to me to break my family's cycle of alcoholism and not pass it on to the next generation. I don't want to look back and regret the choices I have made as an adult.

And so the next stage of my journey began—my journey to complete physical and emotional sobriety.

My Rocky Road to Recovery continued ..

Emotional sobriety

A FTER I FINISHED writing the last sentence of the first draft, instead of feeling joy of accomplishment, I felt stuck. I wanted to experience recovery on a deeper level and write about that. I started questioning myself on why I didn't feel whole. On the surface, everything seemed fine, but deep inside I felt inadequate and uneasy, as if something was not right. I wanted to find out why. I started my quest. God opened new doors for me once again.

First, I found a podcast on healing addictions. Next, I contacted the author of the podcast who turned out to be an Orthodox Christian ordained priest and professional psychotherapist. Almost right away he recognized that I was still holding resentment towards someone and I had a fear of rejection. That was the reason I didn't give up alcohol completely in the past. I didn't really understand the connection and wanted to learn more. He directed me to look into co-dependency and an ACA program (Adult Children of Alcoholics/ Dysfunctional families).

I was intrigued and bought all available ACA literature, downloaded podcast on co-dependency, and dove right in. What I found out was mind boggling. I always suspected there was a connection between my issues and the way I grew up, but I could never put my finger on what exactly happened. Once I read the ACA Laundry List, I realized that most of my issues in my adult life were the result of growing up in an alcoholic, dysfunctional family. After all, besides my grandmother, everyone in my immediate and extended family drank.

I decided to dig deeper.

I contacted Celebrate Recovery (CR) at a local church and went in to see what it was all about. I heard about it before but never actually looked into it. I liked the fact that it was a Christ-based program, similar to all other 12-step programs, but with Christ as Higher Power. I felt I was in the right place when the lady who introduced me to CR said that her goal for joining the program a few years back was to break her family's cycle of dysfunction, so that her son didn't have to grow up and experience what she had to. In the past, I only wanted to recover for God and myself, but this time around, it was different—I wanted to do it for my son and our future generations. I wanted my son to grow up in a loving family, with both parents present. I wanted him to be emotionally and mentally stable, and learn how to deal with life's ups and downs without turning to substances or any other forms of addiction. Of course, I couldn't predict what would happen in the future and if I would even be successful, but at least, I could work on my own character defects and the ways I dealt with life, and prevent subconsciously affecting my child in negative ways.

I learned that physical sobriety alone does not bring emotional sobriety. Our behavior might change for the better once we become physically sober, but certain behavior patterns will stay the same or become worse, like the desire to control everything in everyone, anger, passive-aggressiveness, co-dependency, people pleasing, fear, and so on. I tend to be defensive, passive-aggressive, and controlling, because that's what I learned, growing up. I am also a people pleaser, and I worry about what people think of me. I didn't know why at first. I didn't want to be that way. I also didn't deal with stress in a healthy manner, but took my frustration out on my husband often. I don't even know why he has been dealing with this kind of behavior this long without losing his love for me. I am glad he is paying more attention to my good qualities rather than bad ones. I want to be an example of emotional health for my son. While he is still little and doesn't understand everything that's going on around him, I still have a good chance to re-parent myself, so to speak. I realize full recovery will not happen in one day, if ever at all, but I intend on doing the best I can.

I am ready to stop this generational curse of dysfunction! My son deserves a good home.

I did a psychotherapy evaluation with Father Christoff (inexaustiblecup.org). That's when I discovered that number one issue I had since I was born was the absence of my birth father. My family's alcoholism, combined with being raised by a single mother, led me to most of the bad choices later on in life. I grew up with a distorted view of the world and myself. I decided to continue psychotherapy with Father Christoff and scheduled our next session two weeks from then. All these recent discoveries made me not only curious but also hopeful. Sometimes we don't want to dig deep and face ourselves, but when we find courage and do it, we have a chance for a better, happier, more fulfilling life, not only for ourselves but also for people around us.

In addition to therapy, I made a plan to take a Six-week Challenge at Celebrate Recovery and see where God would lead me. I ended up completing the challenge, joined a 12-Step group, which I ended up quitting because it wasn't the right one for me, but joined ACA group instead. In addition, I auditioned for the worship group, and now I occasionally sing on stage in front of the whole CR gathering! I love going on Friday nights and participate in share groups. Sharing my week's issues or accomplishments definitely makes a huge difference. No numbing of feelings and emotions anymore!

I'm finally completely sober and spend most of my free time learning new things and working on myself. Also, I just found out I'm pregnant again, after twenty months of trying to conceive! God is really great! The more He sees my progress, the more He blesses me! Having another baby just gives me more motivation to be the best version of myself and make my kids and my husband proud! That's my biggest WHY!

What's your WHY?

"*Successful people's lives have shown us over and over again that the quality of our lives is determined not by what happens to us, but rather by what we do about what happens.*" Tony Robbins

P.S. Right before sending this book to my formatter, I gathered enough courage to have an honest conversation with my mom. We talked for five hours straight, where I laid everything that I have been carrying with me in my soul for over twenty years out. She genuinely asked for forgiveness, and we decided to start fresh and rebuild our relationship for the sake of my children and our own healing. I wanted my parents to be a part of my kids' lives, but first, we needed to be honest with each other. To find out more, please visit my blog.

ABOUT THE AUTHOR

K SENIA K. LIVES in Myrtle beach, SC, with her husband, Chris, son, Noah, and their chocolate lab, Roman. Currently, they are expecting another baby. Ksenia has a full-time job. In addition, she is a Certified Integrative Nutrition Health Coach and looking to start her own Life Recovery coaching practice.

Ksenia K. can be contacted at
unstuck.lyl@gmail.com

She would love to hear your honest feedback, questions, suggestions for her next book, or anything related to *Rocky Road to Recovery* that you might want to discuss further.

You can follow her blog at *unstuck.lol* where she shares her weekly struggles and discusses her life recovery further.

Ksenia K. started a Facebook page where she shares daily inspiration www.facebook.com/Unstuck-106123424493691/

Please leave an honest review after purchasing this book. It will mean a lot to her!

Thank you!

RESOURCES

The Fellowship of the Inexhaustible Cup, Father Christoff

WWW.INEXHAUSTIBLECUP.ORG

Adult Children of Alcoholics/Dysfunctional Families

WWW.ADULTCHILDREN.ORG

Alcoholics Anonymous

WWW.AA.ORG

Food Addicts Anonymous

WWW.FOODADDICTSANONYMOUS.ORG

Sexaholics Anonymous

WWW.SA.ORG

Narcotics Anonymous

WWW.NA.ORG

Co-Dependents Anonymous

WWW.CODA.ORG

Anger Addiction

WWW.R-A.ORG

Celebrate Recovery

WWW.CELEBRATERECOVERY.COM

Made in the USA
Coppell, TX
13 May 2021

55645624R00092